Robben Ford:

BLUES**GUITAR** **PHRASING**MASTERY

Create Expressive Blues Guitar Solos with Powerful Phrasing, Articulation & Dynamics

ROBBEN**FORD**

FUNDAMENTAL**CHANGES**

Robben Ford: Blues Guitar Phrasing Mastery

Create Expressive Blues Guitar Solos with Powerful Phrasing, Articulation & Dynamics

ISBN: 978-1-78933-454-8

Published by **www.fundamental-changes.com**

Copyright © 2024 Robben Ford

Edited by Tim Pettingale

www.fundamental-changes.com

Join our free Facebook Community of Cool Musicians

www.facebook.com/groups/fundamentalguitar

Instagram: **FundamentalChanges**

For over 350 Free Guitar Lessons with Videos Check Out

www.fundamental-changes.com

Contents

Introduction

Before I picked up the guitar, my first instrument was the alto saxophone, and in the early part of my musical development I listened to a lot of the great jazz saxophonists. Then, one day a friend introduced me to the music of Miles Davis, playing me some of the album *Sketches of Spain*. I went to the record store to buy my own copy but came away with *Miles Smiles* instead. As far as I was concerned, I was listening to the greatest band I'd ever heard in my life: Miles with Herbie Hancock, Ron Carter, Wayne Shorter and Tony Williams (who was just 18 when the record was made). I fell in love with Miles' music from that moment on.

Fast forward to the mid-1980s and I was living in New York when I received a phone call inviting me to join Miles' band for a run of shows. To say this came as an unexpected shock would be a massive understatement! It blew my mind. But, of course, I said yes.

The first gigs were a run of double-headers with B.B. King. The plan was that some nights B.B. would open and Miles would follow, and other nights they'd flip it around and B.B. would open for Miles.

Before the first show, I have to say I was terrified. Miles had a habit of intimidating the people around him, right off the bat. His very first thing was to try and rattle you and make you feel uncomfortable. He did it because he didn't want people fawning over him; he wanted to know that you were capable of hanging with him without being phased.

But I could see that other people in his orbit *were* kind of afraid of him, so that didn't help or reassure me! The one thing I did know is that I couldn't continue being tied in knots night after night, so I took a long hard look in the mirror and had some strong words with myself.

One night we were due to play at the renowned Beacon Theater in New York. I lived close by, so I walked to the gig, and on the way decided that I would act as if I'd been in Miles' band forever. That night, I threw all my worries aside and played my heart out – perhaps even going a little over the top. During one of my solos I started quoting Hendrix's *Purple Haze* and wondered if I'd gone too far, but then I caught Miles watching me from the side. He had this wide grin on his face and was nodding his approval. I went on to have an amazing time in his band, and the run of shows culminated in a wonderful concert at the 1986 Montreux Jazz Festival, which you can still find on YouTube.

The big lesson I learned from this is that I am who I am, and I do what I do, and I'm happy with that. In other words, just make your music man, and be yourself! And that's the biggest lesson I want to pass along to you in this book.

Here we are going to break down and learn several solos that I played. Each solo has been carefully edited, so that you can learn a collection of the shorter and longer phrases that make up my musical vocabulary. But we're not just learning licks here, because there's so much more to soloing than that. Each idea is explained in detail, so that you can take away a set of tools and ideas to use creatively in your own playing. Ultimately, I want you to find your own voice and play the way you want to play, being comfortable with who you are and what you do, and this book is about equipping you to do that. I want to pass on as much advice as I can to set you on the right path.

Because my inspiration comes from both blues and jazz, here we will look at a range of tunes that include both straight-ahead blues and funky modal fusion. I trust this spectrum of music will open up plenty of new ideas for you to explore in your playing.

I hope you enjoy the journey!

Robben

Get the Audio

The audio files for this book are available to download for free from **www.fundamental-changes.com**. The link is in the top right-hand corner. Click "Download Audio" and choose your instrument. Select the title of this book from the menu, and complete the form to get your audio.

We recommend that you download the files directly to your computer (not to your tablet or phone) and extract them there before adding them to your media library. If you encounter any difficulty, we provide technical support within 24 hours via the contact form.

For over 350 free guitar lessons with videos check out:

www.fundamental-changes.com

Join our free Facebook Community of Cool Musicians

www.facebook.com/groups/fundamentalguitar

Tag us for a share on Instagram: **FundamentalChanges**

Chapter One – Blues Shuffle

We begin our journey by looking at soloing ideas over a tune I wrote called *White Rock Beer…8 Cents*. When I composed this tune, I had in mind the influence Eric Clapton had on my playing – specifically the work he did on the album *Blues Breakers* by John Mayall, released in 1966 and known by guitar players the world over as "the Beano album" (because the cover photo features Eric reading a copy of the classic British kids' comic book *The Beano*).

Clapton was only 21 years old when this record appeared and it just blew everyone's minds. One of the standout tracks is a cover of the Freddie King tune *Hideaway* and Eric kills it. The album signaled a sea change in the electric blues playing of the day – it was an entirely different sound and a different approach. *White Rock Beer* comes out of that tradition.

This tune follows a standard 12-bar blues format in the key of E. There are no real surprises in the chord changes – it's a straight-up blues shuffle. The harmonic twists come from the melodic ideas I played over it. In the first half of this chapter, we'll look at a breakdown of the ideas I played over four choruses of the blues. Then, at the end of the chapter, you'll learn another complete solo over *another* four choruses.

The 12-bar shuffle is one of the most popular vehicles for the blues, so it's essential to know how to navigate it. Here you'll learn plenty of creative ideas to take away and develop further on your own. Let's get into it…

In Example 1a, we start with a question and answer line with a twist.

No doubt you're familiar with the idea of question and answer phrasing, as it's one of the main storytelling devices that all blues players use. We play an opening statement (the question) followed by a similar phrase (the answer). Sometimes the phrases will use the same notes but be played in a different register, and sometimes they'll use different notes but be rhythmically similar. Either way, the point is to create vocal-like phrases that sound like we're having a conversation.

Here, we're playing over an E7 chord, which has the notes E (root), G# (3rd), B (5th) and D (b7). The question phrase begins with a surprise by playing an F# note and bending it up a half step to G. That's moving from the 9th of the chord to the #9 – an unexpected tension to open with.

The answer phrase uses different notes but similar phrasing. Here we're bending from the major 6th (C#) to the b7 (D) of the E7 chord.

We end this phrase in bar four with some standard pentatonic phrasing, but the interesting note choices and tensions of the opening phrases help the listener notice that there's something a little more sophisticated going on here.

Example 1a

In the next example we're playing over the transition from the IV chord (A7) back to the I chord (E7). In bars 1-2, I play another question and answer phrase, but here the answer is more of a development of the motif played in bar one, and I stayed in the same zone of the neck.

As electric blues evolved as a style, it was in the development of the Chicago sound that we first heard jazz-style chord voicings used in the blues, and especially the dominant 9th. This extended note added a different color to the common blues vocabulary.

So, in bar one of Example 1b, we start by highlighting the 9th. All the notes come from the E Minor Pentatonic scale (E G A B D), but it's the effect of that B note over the A7 chord that creates the interest and implies an A9 sound.

In bar two we play a *Hideaway*-inspired phrase that continues to focus on the 9th color tone. First, we reference the b7 and the root of the A7, as well as the 9th, in the hammer-on/pull-off phrase. Then, this is followed by a blues curl (a slight upward bend notated as a 1/4 bend) which pushes the b7 (G) of the A7 chord not quite all the way to the A root note!

From the second half of bar two into bar three, I'm making use of the open high E and B strings to create a pedal tone idea, which ends with a whole step bend up to a B note on the G string. We're now playing over E7 in bar three, so it's a bend to the 5th of the chord.

Example 1b

The great thing about the simplicity of blues harmony is that we can *play* the changes, but we can also just blow over the changes using one scale, based on chord I of the key. When the progression moves from the V chord (B7) to the I (E7), we can outline the difference in the chords, or we can just go right for the I chord's scale. In this example I'm doing the latter.

For the most part, I'm using the E Minor Pentatonic scale to create the melody, but I want to draw your attention to the opening of this example and the double-stop idea in the pickup bar. Here the notes come from the E minor 6 Pentatonic scale – a hybrid pentatonic idea used by fusion guitarists such as John Scofield and others.

The minor 6 pentatonic scale exists within the Dorian scale, from which we extract its five notes. The idea behind the concept is to conjure up the dark, cool mood of the Dorian scale without sacrificing the easy-to-access shapes of the pentatonic scale.

The notes of E Minor 6 Pentatonic, when played over a B7 chord give us some great tensions. The opening E note of the phrase in the pickup bar is the 11th of B7. The open G and B strings are the #5 and root. And the notes at the second fret (A and C#) are the b7 and 9th.

Example 1c

Staying in a Chicago blues state of mind, the next chorus opens with another 9th chord idea. In bar one, the first four notes spell an inversion of E9, beginning on the 5th and omitting the 3rd. The following triplet phrase moves from the b9 (F) of E7 down to the b7. The phrase continues into the beginning of bar two, where the 5th and the root of the chord are emphasized.

One thing you may notice about this line is the phrasing. Because my first instrument was alto sax, and I was influenced by lots of jazz saxophonists (particularly Paul Desmond, Sonny Rollins, John Coltrane and Wayne Shorter), I often think of lines more like a saxophonist than a guitarist.

You can see the evidence of this in the line that starts at the end of bar two and flows into the first beat of bar four. I'll often play lines that start or finish midway through a bar and flow over the bar line. To me, that's approaching phrasing like a saxophonist would, floating over the bar lines rather than being constrained by them. Guitar players often think in blocks of one or two bars, and often start phrases on beat 1. The addition of legato technique here adds to the sax-like quality of the line.

In terms of note choices, this line is built from the E Dorian scale (E F# G A B C# D) which brings a darker color to the idea. I also added in the b5 of the Blues scale (Bb in this case), which acts like a chromatic passing note.

Example 1d

Repetition is a staple idea of all blues players and one that I personally take a lot of pleasure in. It's a simple thing to do, to repeat an idea, but it's very valuable in helping an audience connect what a soloist is playing to what the rest of the band is playing.

If you think about the drummer's job in a band, he's essentially playing the same pattern over and over, adding the occasional fill. There's a lot of repetition! There's no reason why the guitarist can't do that too and, for a while at least, become totally locked into an idea with the rhythm section.

This is the kind of idea I'm hinting at in bars 1-2 of this example, with a simple bend that targets the root note of the A7 chord.

Notice too, in bar three, the idea of playing a low half step bend into the 3rd of the E7 chord.

Example 1e

When playing the next example, especially in bars 1-2, go for a relaxed, behind-the-beat phrasing. Often guitar players are guilty of rushing ahead or pushing the beat. There is a place for this, when we want to create a sense of urgency or momentum. But, especially when playing over a shuffle, we often want to sit back on the beat. Doing this will really help your lines to swing.

The low bend in bar one helps pull back on the beat, where we bend a D note almost to D# with a blues curl, then follow it up with an E note before playing the root of the B7 chord. In bar two, the double-stops with a hammer-on add more power to this bluesy phrase.

In bars 3-4, the ascending triplet run locks into the three feel of the shuffle. The notes are the E Minor Pentatonic scale, apart from the alteration of its G note to G# to outline the major 3rd of the E7 chord.

Example 1f

The ascending run that began in the last bar of the previous example was designed to lead into the higher register idea that starts the next chorus of the tune, and the two should dovetail together.

After the opening hammer-on phrase, this bluesy minor pentatonic lick begins on beat "4&" of bar one, anticipating the first beat of bar two. This lick should be played with plenty of attack. Listen carefully to the audio example to nail the timing and dynamics.

Example 1g

This time, as the progression moves from the IV chord back to the I, we're playing a line punctuated with bends. This idea only uses a few notes, and is all about the articulation.

First, make sure that you are bending the full whole step from D up to E, then later from A up to B. It's important to have great pitch control on your bends to avoid playing phrases that sound unfocused or uncontrolled. Hit the note you are aiming for first and then, if there's time, add vibrato once you're in pitch.

In bar four, the trill idea on the top strings is a way of subtly highlighting the b5 note of the Blues scale.

Example 1h

To end this chorus of the blues, here's an idea that's tied closely to what the rhythm section is playing at this point in the tune. We're using the idea of repetition again to glue it all together.

The triplet lick that is played three times in bars 1-2 is just the E Minor Pentatonic scale, but the G and E notes played over the B7 harmony are ear catching, as they are the #5 and 11th of the chord respectively.

In bar three, be sure to play the bent double-stops with plenty of attack and attitude!

Example 1i

Let's dig into one more chorus of this blues. This line opens with a blues rock idea in bars 1-2, played low down and incorporating the open D string, which is the b7 of the E7 chord.

In bar four, we begin an ascending line that will set up the phrase in bar one of Example 1k. It's a straight 1/16th note run and you'll need to alternate pick this to get it up to speed and play it cleanly. The notes here come from the E Minor Pentatonic scale but I'm augmenting the scale with an additional F# note. F# is the 9th of E7 and evokes that Chicago sound.

The F# note mostly precedes a G note, so here it's functioning like an *approach note* in jazz. In other words, each time it's played its intent is to target an E Minor Pentatonic scale tone. Notice that the F# is never played on a strong down-beat, always on the off-beat, which has the effect of highlighting the strong scale tone that follows.

Example 1j

This line begins with the second part of the run, now descending. For this line, we're playing the E Blues scale (E G A Bb B D). In other words, all the notes of E Minor Pentatonic plus the b5.

As I'm sure you know, the inclusion of the b5 note (Bb) is an integral part of the blues language. It creates its own tension and has its own gravity because it wants to resolve to a scale or chord tone.

Because we're playing the E Blues scale over an A7 chord at this point in the tune, the notes of the scale function as different intervals. Thinking in terms of A7, the E note is the 5th, G is the b7, A is the root, Bb is the b9, B is the 9th and D is the 11th.

Superimposing the E Blues scale over A7 therefore gives us a nice mix of basic chord tones, extended notes, and one altered note, for an instantly more sophisticated sound. (Explore this idea further in your practice session by using the E Blues scale to jam over an A7 chord vamp).

Example 1k

For reference, here's the run that spans examples 1j and 1k isolated – just to help you learn it a little more easily. There's no audio example for this, but use it to plan out the most comfortable fingering approach.

We end this chorus with a question and answer lick over the B7 chord. To make a strong ending statement, we play a stripped-down E7 chord (from low to high, B, D, E, the 5th, b7 and root).

Example 1l

We've looked at four choruses of *White Rock Beer* and explored some different ideas. Next, we're going to word towards you playing a full, four-chorus solo. Blues is a language like any other, and the best way to learn it to begin with is by copying how others speak. As you do, the phrases and ideas that appeal to you get absorbed and begin to form your own way of speaking. Eventually, they inspire you to add your own ideas that are unique to you.

Before we get to the solo, let's break it down into four individual choruses. I'll highlight just a few points of interest in each chorus. After you've learned each 12-bar solo, challenge yourself to join them together and play the full solo.

In this first chorus we'll focus on the idea in bars 9-12.

The phrase over the B7 chord in bars 9-10 uses chromatic approach notes to target chord tones.

First, we bend from a C# note up a whole step to D#, the 3rd of B7. Then, with the bend still held we walk up chromatically on the B string from D# to F# (the 5th of the chord). In bar 10, we walk down chromatically on the D string to target an A note (the b7 of the chord).

At the end of bar ten I'm anticipating the arrival of the E7 chord in bar eleven. Here, I'm visualizing an E9 chord in 7th position and the different color or tension notes that sit around it.

Starting on the D string, 7th fret, we begin this short run on the 11th (A) of E7, followed by the b7 (D) on the G string, and an altered tone (G, the #9) on the B string, 8th fret. After that, we climb chromatically up the high E string on frets 7, 8 and 9. This is another example of chord tone targeting, where the target is the C# note over E7 in bar eleven (the 6th of the chord).

Example 1m

This chorus is all about the articulation of the phrases being played and locking into the shuffle groove we're playing over.

Whenever I start a solo, I almost never play something fast. Instead, I play something melodic and ease my way into it. If you come out with all guns blazing from the start, then you've got nowhere to with your solo. But if you begin with some melodic phrases with plenty of breaths between them, maybe in one register of the fretboard, then you can decide to go higher or lower, to play louder or faster. You have options as to how you want to ramp things up.

Dynamics play a big role and make things more engaging for the listener. In this chorus, I used all kinds of bends to bring a vocal quality to the phrasing. Pay particular attention to the articulation and inject as much emotion as you can into these phrases.

In bar one, I play a quick bend with no vibrato. In bars 2-3, I add some fast vibrato to the whole step bends to create more dynamic phrasing. Then, in bars 6-7 there are controlled blues curls (1/4 note bends). I'm also utilizing open strings here for a more rootsy blues vibe. Then, in bar nine, I aim to get as much feeling as possible out of one note by using different types of bend in the same phrase.

The line ends with a pedal tone idea, bouncing notes off the open high E string to make a shift into the higher register.

Example 1n

The last ascending line of the previous example is targeting a 1/4 bend. Over the E7 chord this is a 9th (F#) to #9 (G) bend, which immediately stands out as something a little different from regular pentatonic language.

This chorus of the solo is all about descending then ascending runs, and in those runs I use rhythmic variation to keep the ideas fresh and slightly unpredictable.

For example, the phrasing of the line that begins on beat "4&" of bar one, and extends to beat 1 of bar three, is saxophone-like and cuts across the beat. On beat 2 of bar two we have an 1/8th note surrounded by 1/16th notes, which breaks up the phrase and makes it a bit more unpredictable. This line is also based around the E Dorian scale, which brings a different flavor compared to the pentatonic/blues scale.

Another phrase to listen carefully to starts at the end of bar three and ends on beat 1 of bar five. When playing this run, you'll start off with 1/8th note triplets, but then on beat 2 of bar four switch gear into straight 1/16th notes to speed the line up.

The line in bars 5-6 does the opposite, starting with ascending 1/8th note triplets, then slowing the phrase down in bar six with a 1/4 note bend.

Play through these runs slowly and first, working out the best fingering, before attempting them at the speed of the recording.

Example 1o

This chorus opens with some short punchy phrases in bars 1-3. Then, a descending triplet run in bar four targets the G chord tone of A7 that falls on beat 1 of bar five. Pay attention to the articulation of the bends in bar six, where the first whole step bend is played slowly and gradually hits pitch.

You might need to spend some time figuring out the fingering and timing of the descending lick in bars 8-9, which uses open strings wherever possible. Incorporating the open strings here helps us to get away from the inevitable stepwise phrases that often characterize the pentatonic scale, so that we play something less obvious.

Example 1p

Having worked your way through the individual choruses of this solo, see if you can put them together and play the full solo. Don't necessarily aim for perfection, however. If you make a mistake, just keep going and see if you can get back on track. You don't need to hit the reset button and start over if you play a wrong note.

Example 1q – "White Rock Beer...8 Cents" – Full Solo

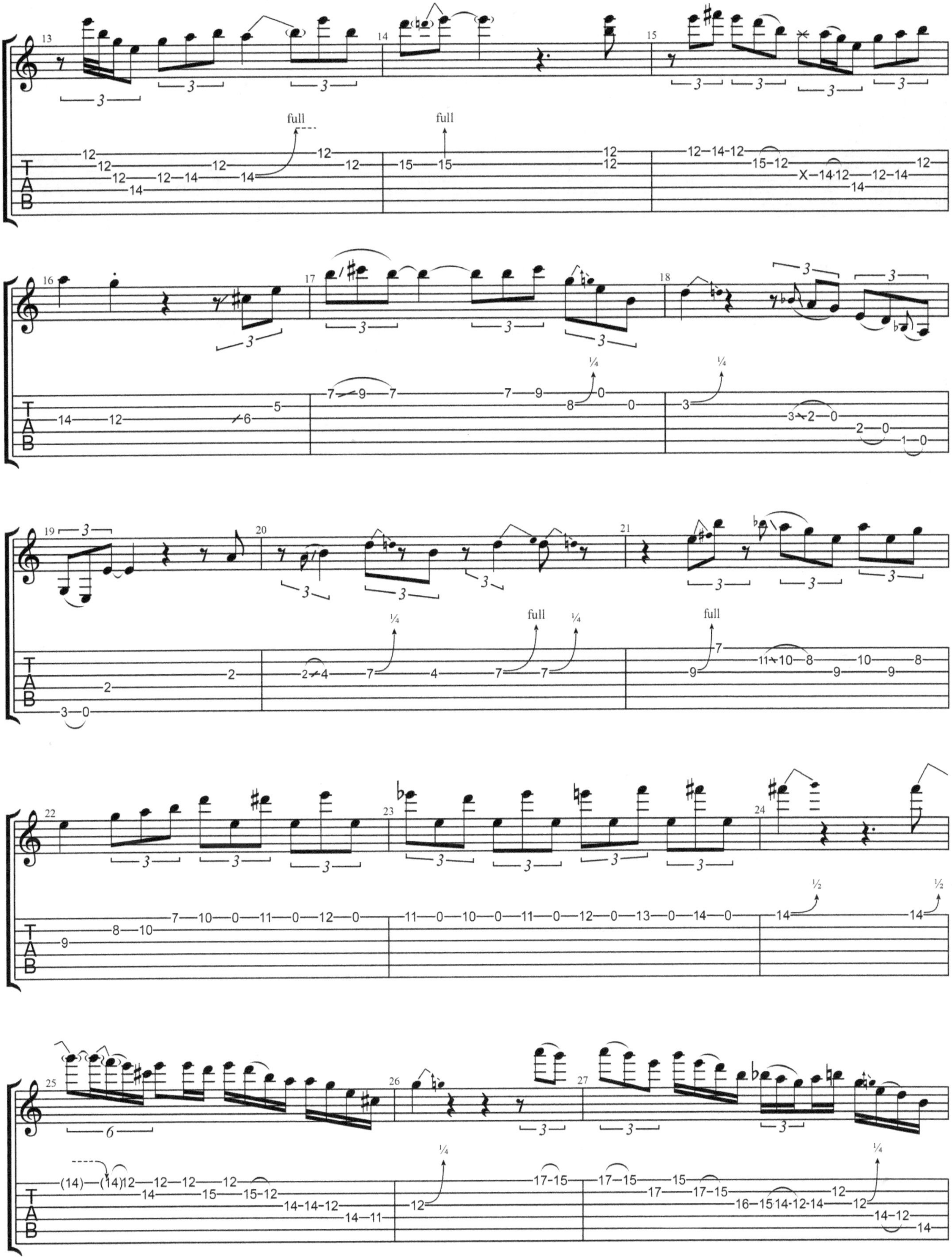
full
full
full
full
TAB

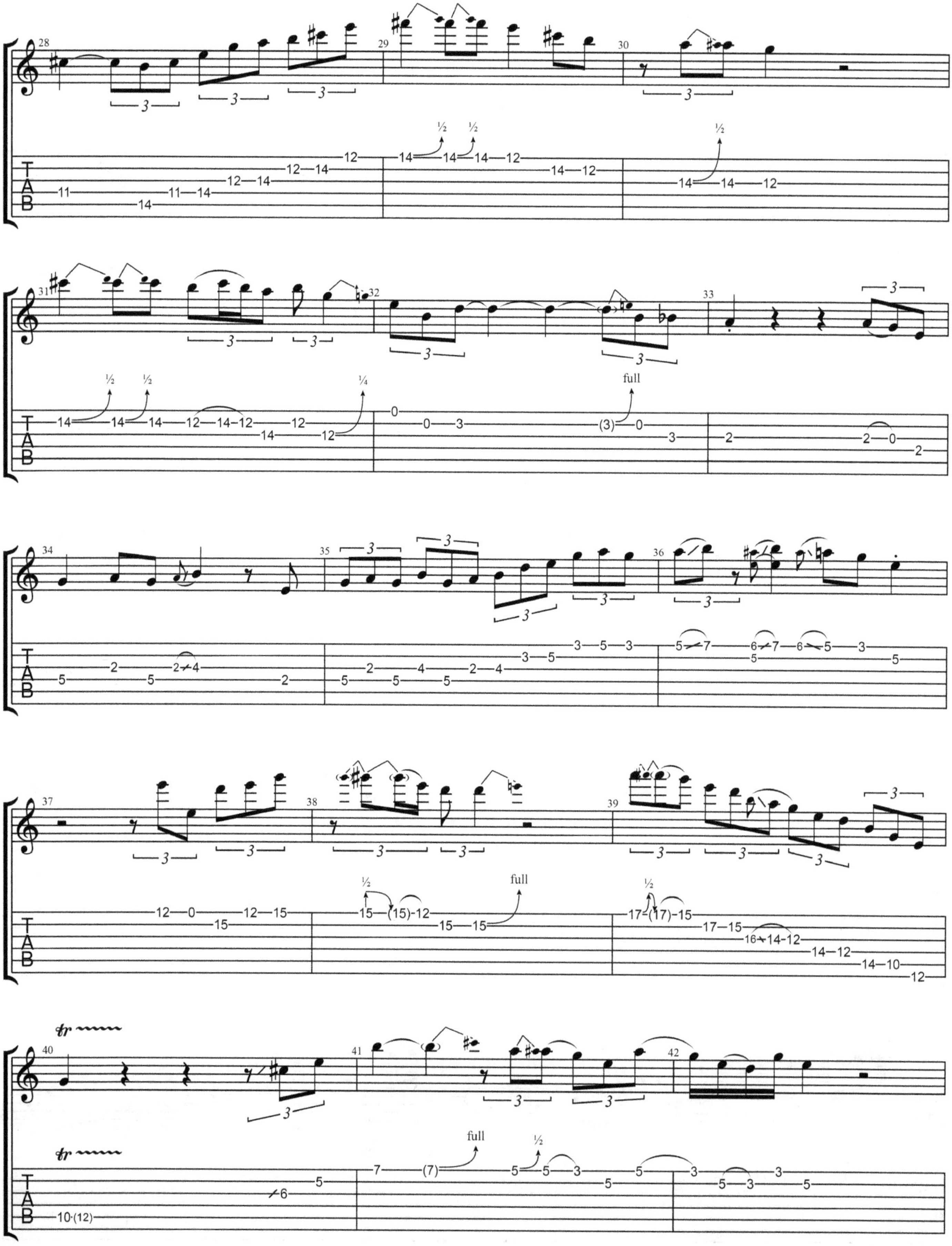
TAB
full
tr

In your audio download you have the backing track loop that I played over. Now I want to challenge you to compose your own solo over this tune. Start by just jamming over it and see what ideas emerge that really appeal to you. Then start over and work on developing some of those ideas.

Next, I urge you to just listen to the backing track and compose a solo in your head, without touching your guitar. When you "hear" something you like, work on transferring it from your head onto your instrument. We have a lot of wonderful tools for learning guitar these days, but your ears are your best friends when it comes to making soulful, spontaneous music.

If you haven't developed your ear, then you'll rely on technique and the catalog of licks that you know. But your long term goal is to move away from playing one lick after another and to get to the place where you can hear a note in your head and instantly play it.

Listening and then mimicking (whether you're copying what someone else played or repeating an idea you just heard in your head) is a really important part of your development as a musician. So, learn the language and copy ideas, but above all *listen well!*

Chapter Two – Funky Blues Modal Vamp

The blues is a great canvas for getting creative. Its simple three-chord structure leaves a lot of space for personal expression and allows us to add our own unique vocabulary. In modern blues, vamps are an equally important vehicle for improvisation – in other words, tunes that have extended sections that stay on just one or two chords.

Vamps are often ii – V movements that don't resolve (Em7 – A7, for example) or they can be modal i.e., moving between seemingly unrelated chords.

I wrote the tune *Go* as a funky, fusion-oriented vamp. It can be considered a modal tune, but there is an internal logic to the chord changes.

First, we have eight bars of a C7 vamp, before we shift down to A7 for four bars – an interval of a minor 3rd. The minor 3rd shift is a common movement in jazz and funk, and you can shift up or down.

From the A7 chord, we then move down a whole step to G7 for four bars (including a run up from E minor) and here the G7 is functioning like a V chord to resolve back to the I (C7).

Learning to navigate the minor 3rd shift is a great skill to have, as it comes up often in blues and jazz, so here we'll look at different ways of flowing seamlessly between those chords. Before we look at some melodic ideas, however, I'd like to show you a few rhythm guitar ideas that I'd play on a tune like this.

Amongst my early guitar influences were Jimi Hendrix and Steve Cropper. Hendrix tends to be remembered for his blistering soloing technique, but of course he was a consummate rhythm player. Then I was exposed to the grooving side of rhythm and blues, and the amazing rhythm parts laid down by Cropper.

In the beginning, I was not a good rhythm guitar player – I didn't really have a clue what it was all about! But, eventually it clicked, especially when I observed that drummers and bass players tended to lay down repetitive patterns that grooved and locked in with one another.

When we think about rhythm playing, first and foremost it's important that we play a supportive part – one that dovetails with the other musicians. Repetition is an important tool in achieving this but that doesn't mean our parts have to be boring. We can stand out by using chord voicings that bring some interest to the harmony.

So, rather than playing standard voicings of C7, A7 and G7, and sticking to them, in the rhythm examples that follow you'll see that I like to think in terms of extended chord voicings that have more interesting tensions.

However, instead of playing the full chords, I tend to break them down and play smaller fragments. This has two advantages: first, the smaller voicings cut through in the mix more than large voicings with lots of notes. Second, from those small voicings it's much easier to create little riff ideas and chord-phrases.

Rhythm Ideas

In this first example, I'm visualizing a four-note C9 chord voicing at the 7th fret. The guitar is a shape-oriented instrument, and you may notice this looks like the shape for an Em7b5, if you know your jazz voicings. But if we were to add a C bass note to that shape we'd have a full C9 voicing. So, it's a C9 without a root note, and when the bass player is holding down the root, that's the sound we hear.

Mostly we're playing just three notes of the chord and we have space to add a couple of notes around it. When playing a funky part like this, keep your picking hand moving up and down constantly, and control when you make contact with the strings.

Here, I'm strumming a 1/16th note pattern, so each bar is counted:

"1-e-&-a-**2**-e-&-a-**3**-e-&-a-**4**-e-&-a"

It's the job of the fretting hand to control when the chords sound and when you hear only a percussive rhythm. Lightly lift the fingers of the fretting hand to get the percussive chugs, and lift the strumming hand away from the strings when you just want to leave space.

Example 2a

Bars two and four of this example contain a couple of RnB-style rhythm licks, inspired by the kind of thing Steve Cropper or Curtis Mayfield might play.

In bar three, the chord voicing on the top strings could be seen as part of a larger C9 voicing, but leaving out the bottom two strings, it can also be understood as a C7sus2 chord. It's a classic funk voicing that cuts beautifully through a mix. Be careful to control your strumming/muting action, and ensure the chord lands right on beat 2.

Example 2b

Now the chord progression modulates down a minor 3rd to A7. Here is quite an understated rhythm part that uses a suspended sound to create a riff.

I'm visualizing the same 9th chord shape as before, now moved down to the 4th fret. This time, I've stripped it down even more and most of this rhythm part is played using just two notes. The riff idea is to play G and D notes (respectively the b7 and suspended 4th of A7) then resolve the D note to C#, so we have a sus4 moving to the 3rd of A7.

Example 2c

Here's another C7-based idea for when the tune modulates back up. The first part of this idea is based around a standard C9 voicing at the 3rd fret. First, we slide into the shape from below and, again, we're stripping it down to two notes. We're following the same suspended riff idea as the previous example, but this time in reverse, going from the 3rd to the sus4. I also move the chord's Bb note (b7) down to an A (6th) briefly.

A 9th chord with a suspended 4th is a great voicing for funky rhythm playing on a vamp and has a much more interesting sound than a regular dominant 7 voicing. In bar three we're targeting the C9sus4 chord chromatically from above. From low to high, this voicing is built from the b7 (Bb), 9th (D), sus4 (F) and root (C).

In bar four, that unusual chord shape is a C7 triad inversion with the root note in the middle. It's an idea I like to use because it captures the sound of C7, but the way the intervals are arranged give it a chiming, even slightly dissonant sound, which comes from placing two notes a whole step apart on adjacent strings.

Example 2d

You could think of this next rhythm part as another "suspended" idea. This time, however, rather than moving one note, we're achieving the effect by moving a three-note chord by a whole step. Played at the 10th fret, this shape is a C6. Moved down two frets, the same shape becomes a C7sus2.

This is one of those ideas you can just "discover" on the guitar. You might play something like this by accident, when you're just exploring sounds (which you should do often, if you don't do so already). You know it sounds right, so it is right! You can figure out the theory of why it works later.

Example 2e

Next, more ideas for the A7 section of the tune. To bring contrast and interest to this rhythm part, I started with our now-familiar A9 voicing on the middle strings, and to take it somewhere, moved out onto the top strings and into a higher zone of the fretboard.

Knowing your fretboard is a really important factor in being able to create chord-phrases like this, spelling out the harmony in different areas of the neck. Players like Kurt Rosenwinkel, a long-time favorite of mine, say that when they see a chord like A7 on a chart, at that moment the whole neck is A7 to them. They can "see" A7 clusters all over the fretboard, then pick out the sounds they want to make.

There are lots of free fretboard mapping tools available online to help with this task. Try typing in all the notes of an A9 and then explore the resulting map. As you do, you'll discover recurring shapes across the neck and lots of "hidden" clusters of notes that lend themselves to playing more interesting rhythm parts.

At the end of bar four here we transition chromatically into one of the G7 sections of the tune.

Example 2f

For the G7 bars, here is a subtle strummed part. In bars 1-2, this little four-note voicing is a neat way of expressing the colorful sound of a G13 chord with the root note located on top. The other notes (from high to low) are the 13th, 3rd and b7. This is a way of playing all the important chord tones to create the sound, without playing a cumbersome barre chord.

Bar three is a kind of turnaround to get us back to the C7 vamp. There's another minor 3rd shift here, from E7 to G7, which wants to resolve back to C7.

Example 2g

Back with the C7 vamp, here's a rhythm part that uses repetition. Listen carefully to the audio example to pin down the timing of when the chords sound, because most are played on the offbeat. If you count the bars in 1/8th notes ("1-&-2-&-3-&-4-&"), the chords are nearly all on the "&". The key is to keep the picking hand strumming down and up in 1/16th notes and using the fretting hand to control popping out the chord stabs.

In bar four, the Db9 is a sidestep movement to create a little tension before resolving back to C9.

Example 2h

This example begins with a palm-muted two-note chord idea. Muting the strings slightly just brings a new flavor to the idea, and we're using variations of C chords to create interest.

At the end of bar four we have a louder strummed chromatic descent to get us from the C7 to the A7 section.

Example 2i

Using two-note voicings makes it easier for us to add embellishment notes around the shapes and to move around the fretboard more quickly. However, there are times when we want to hold down a larger chord shape and just isolate certain groups of notes, or individual notes.

In bar two, there is an unusual chord voicing that demonstrates the duality of certain guitar chords. That is to say, many of our four-note voicings on guitar can represent different chords depending on the musical context, especially what bass note is being played underneath.

For example, we've already discovered that a C9 chord without its root note looks/sounds exactly like an Em7b5. If we play that shape over a C bass note, it will sound like C9. If we play it over an E bass note, it will sound like Em7b5.

Similarly, here we have what guitar players will recognize as a common GMaj7 shape (place your index finger on the 2nd fret of the high E string, then allow the rest of your fingers to fall onto the adject strings at the 3rd, 4th and 5th frets).

We've all played this shape many times as a GMaj7, but place an A bass note underneath it and we get a colorful sounding Asus13 chord. From low to high the intervals are the b7, 9th, sus4 and 13th. The bass player provides the A root note that creates this context.

Hold down this chord for the first part of bar two, then release it when the note on the B string needs to move.

Example 2j

You can experiment with these rhythm ideas over the backing track provided in your audio download. Now let's move on to explore some melodic ideas over this tune. At the end of the chapter, my full solo is transcribed, but we'll break it down and look at the ideas in isolation.

Solo breakdown

It's tempting, when starting to improvise over a vamp-based track like this, just to play a series of licks that you know will work. But that can sound formulaic, and there's so much more to crafting a solo than that.

It's good to have a vocabulary of ideas ready to use – that's a great asset. The bigger the vocabulary the more we'll have to say. After that, it's all about how we apply the ideas and express them to our audience. We want to tell a story with our improvisation.

Way back, I had the good fortune of being invited to join Tom Scott's band The L.A. Express. I received a call from Tom, who I didn't know at the time, asking me if I would join his group to replace Larry Carlton, and to go on tour with Joni Mitchell.

I had been working with Jimmy Witherspoon for a couple of years and wanted to get back to developing my solo career, so initially I said no! Thankfully, Tom persuaded me to get involved by playing me the album *Court and Spark*, which hadn't yet been released and was still in acetate form. It was beautiful, sophisticated music and I was drawn in.

My time with that band taught me a huge amount about the craft of musicianship, especially listening to Tom, and also my good friend the keyboardist Roger Kellaway. Roger was fond of saying, "There's a lot of music to be made in the key of C." In other words, just the white notes.

I would say, there's a lot of music to be made from the pentatonic scale. Having a large musical vocabulary doesn't mean knowing endless exotic scales – we can have a great vocabulary by taking something simple and applying it well.

The opening bars of the solo start with a couple of phrases that are allowed plenty of space to breath, followed by a saxophone-like phrase that spans the end of bar three into bar four.

Throughout, I'm using the C Minor Pentatonic scale (C Eb F G Bb), but occasionally I "borrow" a note from another scale for a particular effect. In bars two and four, you'll see that I borrowed the b5 note (Gb) from the C Blues scale. And, at the end of bars two and five, I borrowed the A note from the C Major Pentatonic scale.

The blues curls in bar three, and the hammer-ons/pull-offs in bar four, add character to the phrasing.

Example 2k

Here's a simple phrase that includes some chromatic passing notes. We touched on the idea of approach notes in the previous chapter – a concept used more in jazz than blues. Simply put, the idea is to target chord tones or scale tones, approaching them from above or below.

Take the middle phrase of bar one. Here we approach an E note (the 5th of C9) from a half step below. Then, starting from the C root note, we play a chromatic B note to get to b7 (Bb) of the chord.

In bar two, this phrase is all C Major Pentatonic, but the first note is approached from a half step below with a chromatic note.

Example 2l

The next idea over the C9 section is a funky, in-the-pocket type line. Here we are using the C Mixolydian scale (C D E F G A Bb) to capture the sound of the C9 chord, and rhythmically we're tightly locked into the groove.

In bar two, a nice way to play the b7 (Bb) of the scale is to bend into it from the 6th (A) a half step below. In this bar, we also bend from a non-scale tone (Eb) to the 3rd (E). In bar three, we jump back to C Minor Pentatonic for the final phrase.

Example 2m

Here the tune modulates to A7 and we switch to the A Mixolydian scale to play this line, which has the notes A B C# D E F# G.

After the initial phrase, in bar two we spell out the sound of an A13 chord, playing it in broken-up 6th intervals. A13 is an extended dominant chord that contains the notes A, C#, E, G, B, D and F#.

The wide 6th interval on guitar always contain a string skip. Often, both notes are plucked together, country guitar style, but they can also be staggered as they are here. At the beginning of bar two we pair up the 3rd (C#) and root (A) of the chord, a 6th interval apart, then we pair the 9th (B) and the b7 (G), and so on, as we work our way through the chord.

Example 2n

This line highlights the bluesy aspect of A Mixolydian by adding double-stops and half step bends. Listen to the audio to capture the articulation of the phrasing.

Example 2o

Bar two of the previous line began a transition into the G7 section of the tune and examples 2o and 2p can be considered one complete line, separated out here for clarity. In Example 2p we've switched to G Mixolydian for this part of the line (G A B C D E F).

The challenge when changing the scale to fit the chord, as we move from one chord to the next, is to do so as seamlessly as possible, as though the phrase was always meant to be. We don't want to sound as though we're just jumping from one chord to the next in an obvious fashion.

This process just takes time, as we play more and more, and develop a stronger visualization of the notes on the fretboard. Eventually, we can become more adept at "joining the dots" and learn to move between scales using the next closest note.

Example 2p

Here's an example of how we might achieve that kind of seamless transition. We know that we're going to move from a G7 tonal center to C7. We can pick a starting note to launch from and a target note that we want to land on – now all we need is a vehicle to get us from point A to point B!

If you know my playing, you'll know that I often use the Diminished scale. This is a symmetrical scale built from alternating half steps and whole steps (or whole steps and half steps, depending on where you start from). It's also an octatonic scale, meaning that it contains eight tones instead of the usual seven.

Here, I'm playing the E Half-Whole Diminished scale as the harmony moves from E minor to G and into C7. The run starts on the last note of bar two.

E Half-Whole Diminished contains the notes E F G G# Bb B C# D and you'll see that this a straight run up the scale. What's interesting about the scale is that it contains a great mix of inside and outside notes, so that we hear some chord tones in there, but also some tension notes.

At the end of bar two, I play a chromatic Eb note to get to the E target note I had in mind, the 3rd of C9.

Example 2q

Here is another line built from the C Mixolydian scale. To make the line more interesting, I added a couple of Eb approach notes. Each of these is played with a slide into the E note that follows (the 3rd of C9). A great way of extending a line is to play repeating notes and you'll find that idea used here. The result is a long, sax-like phrase played mostly with 1/16th notes, but I deliberately broke up the line by adding in 1/16th note rests.

Example 2r

The next section opens with a C Minor Pentatonic phrase in bars 1-2. Some articulation is added with 1/4 and 1/2 note bends. The first two are country style bends, where we hold the note on the high E string and push the note on the B string slightly sharp with a blues curl.

In bar three, we're again using the idea of extending the line by adding Eb approach notes before each E chord tone. In bar four, the descending run launches from an A note and is targeting the root of the A9 chord in bar five.

Example 2s

The low riff that opens this A7 section has a pentatonic sound to it, but uses notes from A Mixolydian. We continue to use that scale to create a melodic line in bars 3-4 and end with an A9 inverted arpeggio. This final six-note phrase turns into a motif, which we'll continue at the beginning of Example 2u.

Example 2t

In bar one, we continue the arpeggio motif. Here, we've adapted it for the G9 chord, actually playing a G11 arpeggio twice, first played from root, then from the b7.

The descending run in bar two uses a new scale idea. The notes come from the G Mixolydian Bebop scale (G A B C D E F F#), which is an eight-note scale identical to G Mixolydian, but with the addition of a passing chromatic note placed between the b7 and root note.

Jazz musicians pioneered the use of bebop scales as the modern jazz artform developed. Scales typically have seven notes, but in jazz it's very common to play long passages of 1/8th notes, so it made sense to add a passing note to turn any scale into an eight-note scale. There are also major and minor bebop scales as well as this dominant chord version.

Example 2u

Now we transition out of the G7 section back to the C7 section. Here, we're playing a riff-like motif using double-stops derived from C Mixolydian (except for one at the end of bar four which uses C Minor Pentatonic). This is the kind of idea that makes it easy for your audience to connect with the music, because it's simple, repetitive and very rhythmic.

Example 2v

Next, a line full of articulation that mixes full, half-step and 1/4 note bends. The line combines elements of C Mixolydian and C Minor Pentatonic and just flows between those scales.

Many of the note choices are mixolydian, but then I'll just hear a different sound in my head that I want to play and I'll add in that different color to the picture I'm trying to paint. It turns out that I'm frequently bending the D note of the mixolydian up a half step to the Eb note of the minor pentatonic, but that wasn't really a conscious decision – it's just the sound I heard in my head, transferred onto the guitar. Sometimes you just have to feel your way through a line and it almost plays itself!

Example 2w

This descending run with chromatic notes starts from the root of the A7 chord and is heading for the target of hitting the 3rd of A7 in bar two, played with a bluesy double-stop lick. To make the line sound more fluid and interesting, I added some sliding articulation between the notes. You could play most of this with one finger to exaggerate the effect.

Example 2x

The previous example ended with a blues-rock style chordal idea over the G7 section and we continue that theme over the first couple of bars here. Even though we're still playing over G7, in bars 3-4 we switch to using C Mixolydian ideas, anticipating the change to C7, which creates some brief tension and resolution.

Example 2y

You've practiced the whole solo in smaller chunks, now work towards putting it all together to play the full solo. Also, just enjoy jamming along to the backing track and work on developing the lines that really appeal to you.

Example 2z – "Go" – Full Solo

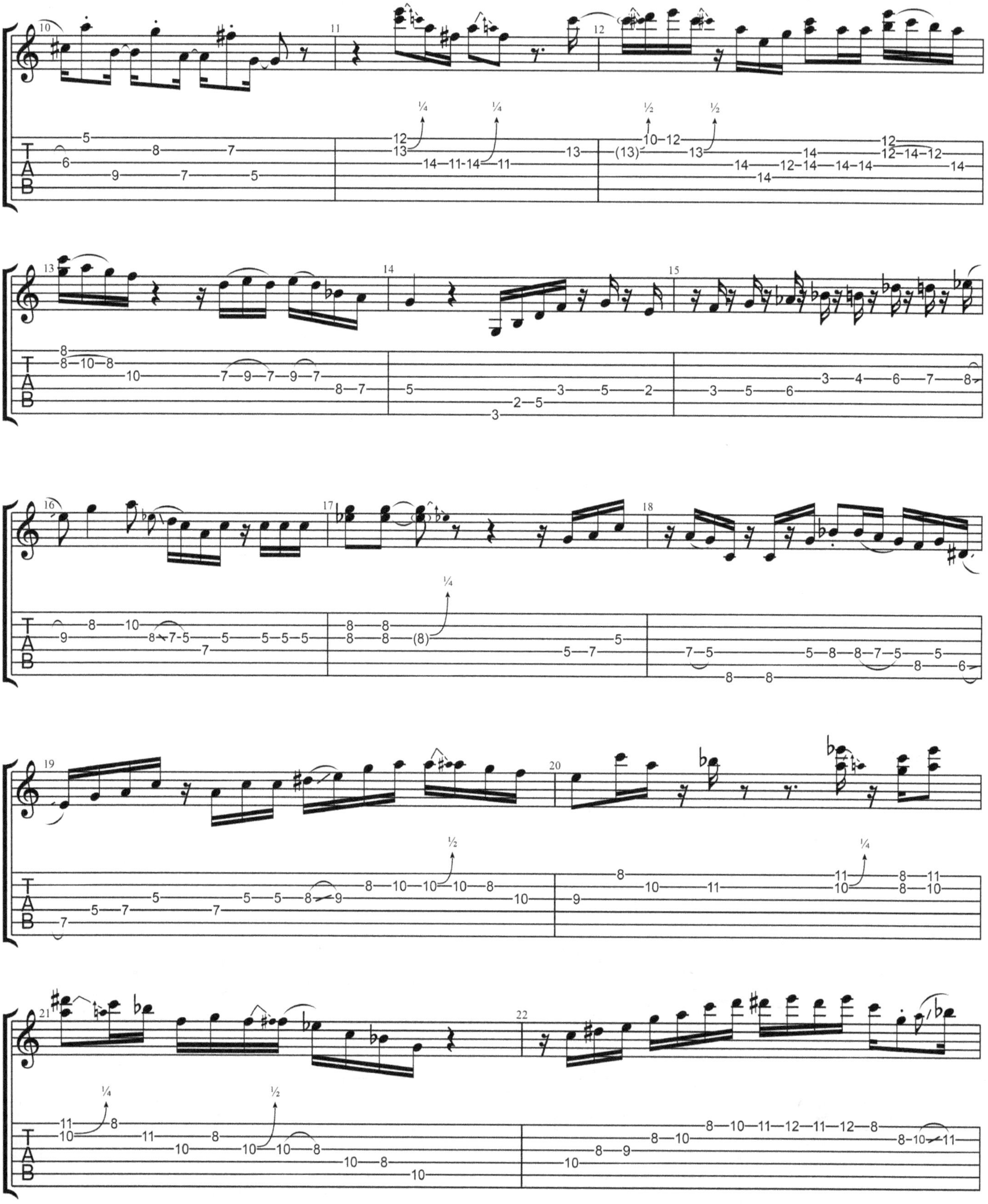

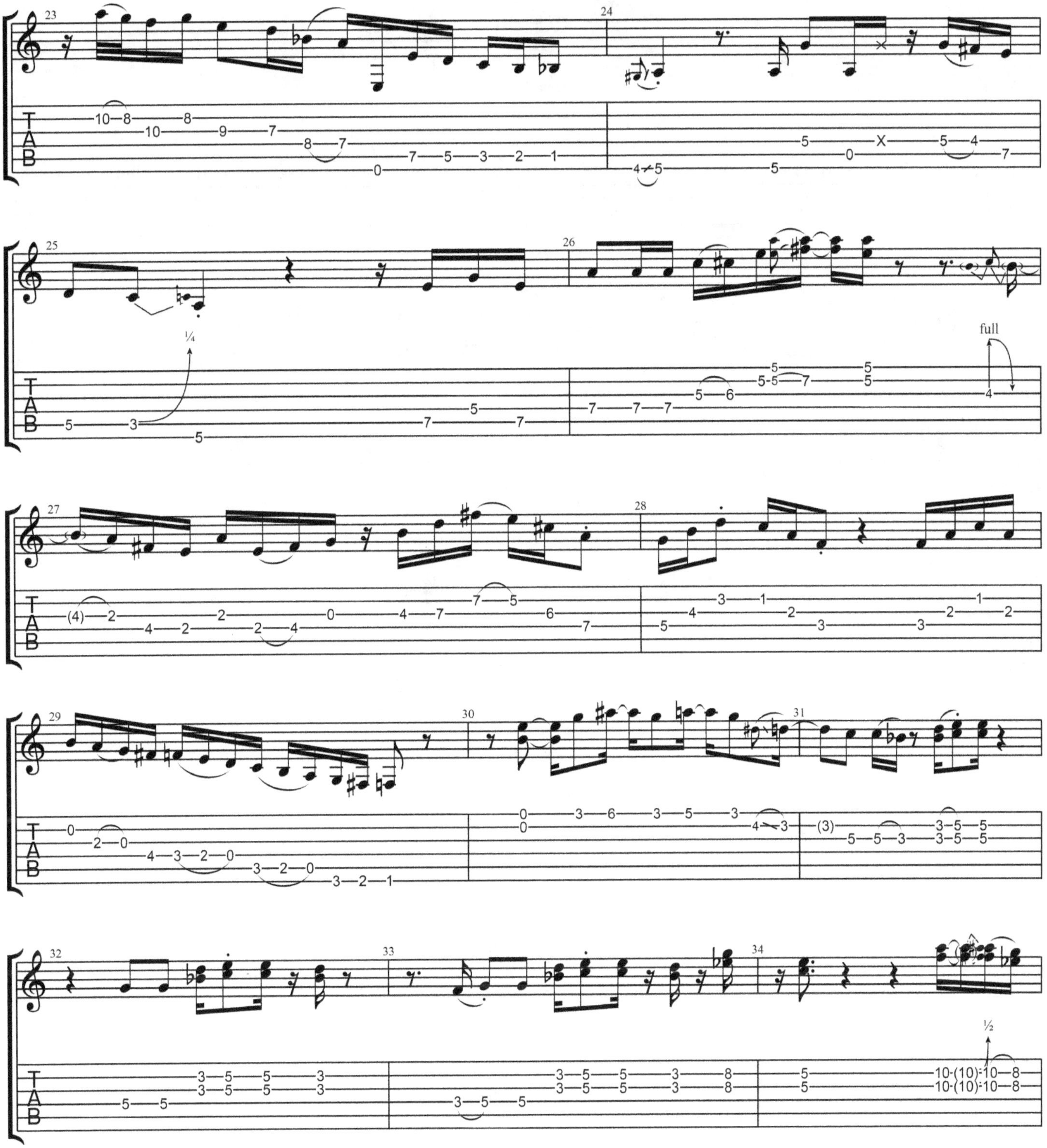
full

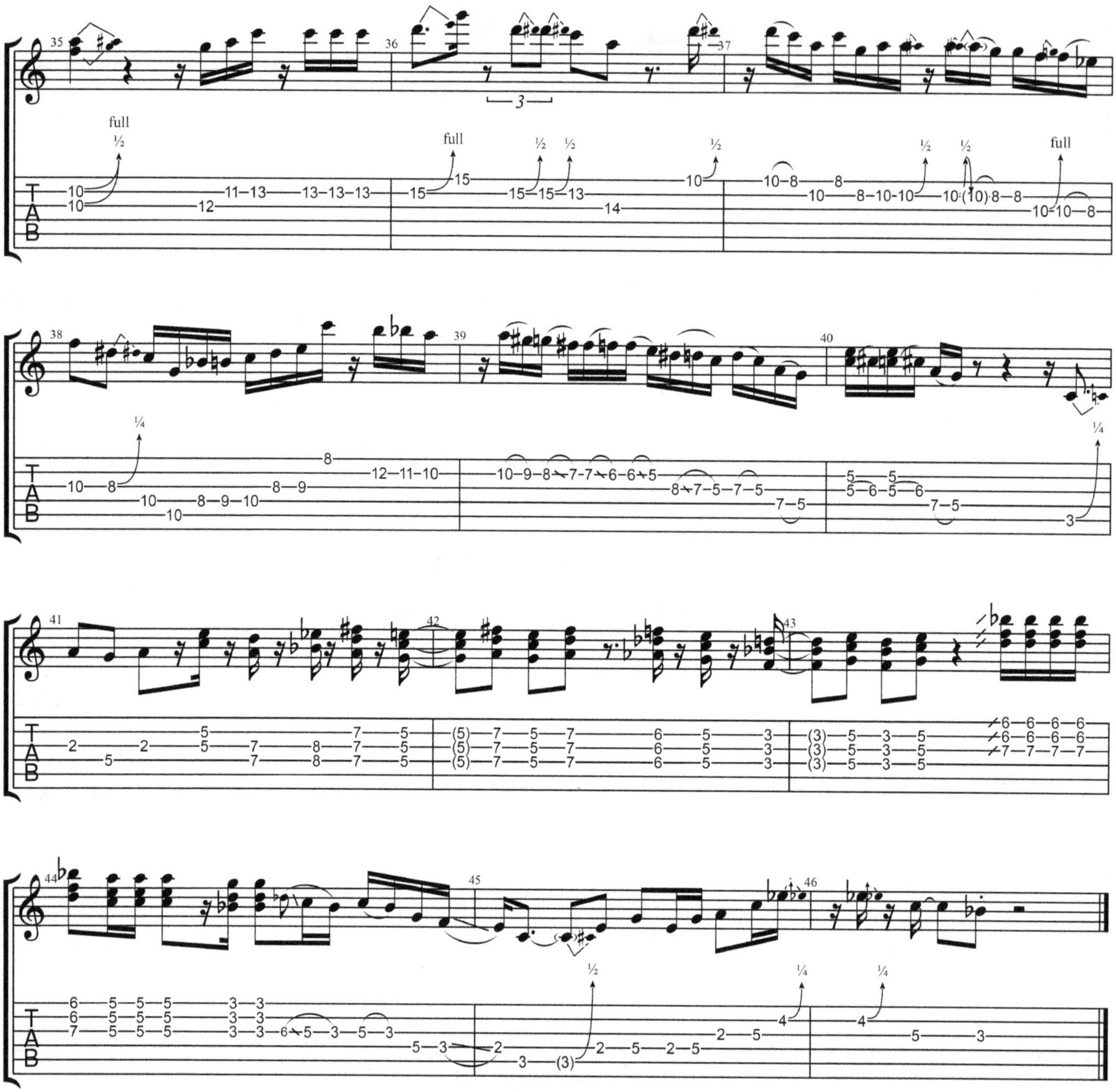
full
½
¼
TAB

Chapter Three – Fusion Vamp

In this chapter we're going to look at another modal tune, a composition of mine called *A Dragon's Tail*. We've explored dominant chord vamps and now we'll work on a minor chord vamp. There are lots of bars of Am7 here, and we'll use different A Minor related scales to improvise over them.

Occasionally, a bridge section moves into F11 to Ebmaj7 chord changes. This is a modal leap and a shift away from the A Minor harmony, so we'll need a different strategy for soloing over this section, and to make our lines flow seamlessly between these two tonalities.

The opening statement for this solo uses the A Dorian scale (A B C D E F# G). The Dorian gives us a slightly darker or cooler sound than the straight minor scale. Twice here I use a melancholy sounding half step bend from the 6th (F#) to the b7 (G) of the A minor chord. It's not a common bend, so it stands out as something a little different.

The final phrase of bar four uses the notes C, B, G and E to make the sound of an Am9. There's no root note, but the notes are the b3, 9th, b7 and 5th respectively, which perfectly describe the chord.

Example 3a

The opening eight-note phrase here uses the A Minor Pentatonic scale. Although there are several notes grouped together on adjacent strings, you'll notice that these don't really represent an Am chord shape – they are just a cluster of notes that sit within the scale pattern. This idea comes from viewing the whole neck as A Minor Pentatonic at this moment, and having a deep familiarity with its intervals. This is better explained using a neck diagram that maps the scale across the fretboard:

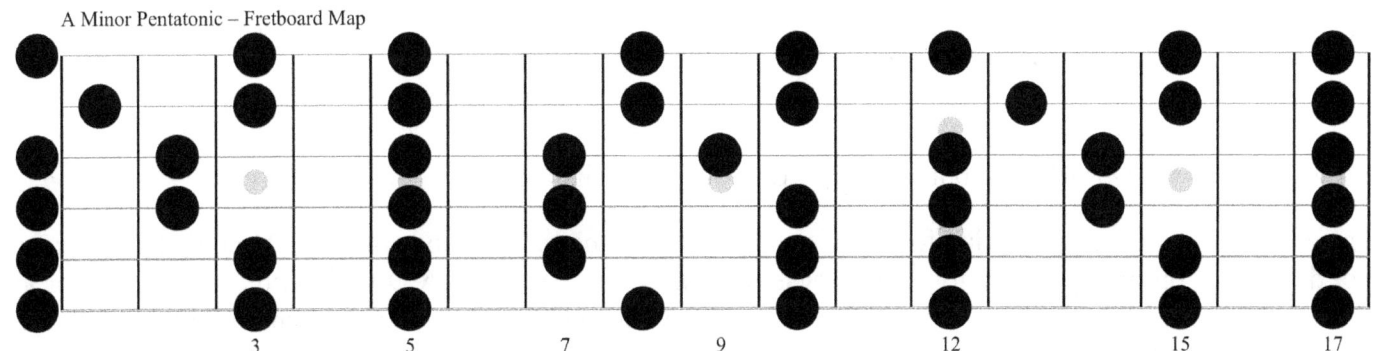

A Minor Pentatonic – Fretboard Map

Once you begin to understand the scale in this way, you can start to break out of predictable patterns and play fresh ideas. Here, we view the scale as one big pattern, rather than a series of smaller box shapes that must then be connected together.

The box shapes are useful to help us learn the scale with easy fingerings that cover the fretboard. But, while you should definitely learn it across the whole neck, it's good to do so in a way that doesn't leave you locked into those patterns.

It's more valuable to train your ears to *know* the scale and anticipate each note you play. This will really give you the freedom to play the scale from any point on the fretboard. I'm sure many guitar teachers would raise an eyebrow at some of my fingerings because I'm doing the equivalent of finger painting on guitar: just going wherever I feel. But that comes out of a deep relationship with the scale.

Also notice here the use of the A Blues scale (A C D Eb E G) for the line in bar three. Whenever we use the minor pentatonic scale for this type of music, it's kind of inevitable that we'll add in that b5 note somewhere.

Example 3b

Example 3c uses an advanced idea that you might like to explore if you dig the sound it makes. From bar one to halfway through bar three, this line uses the A Dorian scale. Then you'll notice a Bb note appear in bar three to play a phrase that gives the line a kind of Eastern feel over the A Minor harmony. Over the Am7 chord, the Bb note is the b9 interval, which we consider a pretty tense note for a minor chord.

The scale here is known as the Dorian b2, which has the notes:

A Bb C D E F# G

It's identical to the Dorian scale but contains a Bb note rather than a B.

This scale has its roots in Assyrian folk music and is actually the second mode of the G Melodic Minor scale. So, depending on how you like to view things, you can see this scale as A Dorian with a minor 2nd, or as superimposing G Melodic Minor over an Am7 chord to create a Dorian sound with a tense b9 interval. Either way, it's an idea you might want to experiment with to immediately create a more exotic sound when soloing.

46

Example 3c

The opening phrase of this idea uses another scale color you might consider experimenting with over minor chord vamps. Here, the line is constructed from the notes of A Melodic Minor (A B C D E F# G#). Think of playing a common Am9 voicing at the 5th fret, you'll see that the notes of A Melodic Minor sit around that shape, acting much like approach notes – and they create a nice, quickly resolved tension.

The main melodic idea in this line is to focus on a couple of extended chord tones on the high E string. First, at the 10th fret, the D note implies an Am11 sound. Then the focus shifts to a B note, suggesting an Am9 sound.

The latter half of bar four into bar six is our transition into the bridge section of the tune, where the tonal center will move away from A Minor. Here we'll play a phrase based around 10th position, ending with a fast slide from the note G into A (the G is a grace note, so barely heard).

Example 3d

The first chord of the bridge is an F11. We repeat the fast G to A slide at the beginning of the line. The A note is the 11th interval of F11, and of course the root note of the A minor chord we've been playing over. So, the first strategy you can use when jumping from one tonal center to another is to look for a *common note*, shared by both tonalities, and play it over both chords.

F11 (sometimes written as Eb/F) is an extended dominant chord. Technically, it's an F7 chord with both the 9th and 11th added – so it's a six-note chord, though we normally omit notes to play it more easily on guitar.

The appropriate scale for this chord is F Mixolydian (F G A Bb C D Eb). If we compare this scale to A Dorian you'll see the two scales have several notes in common:

A Dorian: A B C D E F# G

F Mixolydian: F **G A** Bb **C D** Eb

The four common notes are all possibilities to get us from an Am7 chord to F11.

In bar three we change chord again to EbMaj7.

At this point, the question arises, how are these two chords related to one another, and how does the bridge section relate to the A Minor section of the tune?

F7 and EbMaj7 chords both naturally occur in the key of Bb Major (chords V and IV respectively). With this in mind, we can view the whole tune as an A Minor vamp with a half step shift up to Bb Major for the bridge.

In bars 3-4, if you analyze the note choices, you'll see that I just continue playing the F Mixolydian scale. Because F7 and EbMaj7 share the same Bb Major parent key, the notes still fit. When played over an EbMaj7, those notes create a Lydian scale sound.

Example 3e

Ebmaj7

We continue the same strategy over the second half of the bridge, using the F Mixolydian scale to solo over both chords. When the harmony changes back to A Minor, we're using the D note that the two key centers have in common, played at the beginning of bar three as a bend, starting from another common note, C. Then we're back into A Dorian.

Example 3f

F11

Ebmaj7

Am

Now we're back into the A Minor vamp and a blues-rock influenced lick using just the A Minor Pentatonic scale. Make sure you're bending the B string the full whole step to pitch the A note. The familiar idea here is sounding an A on both the B and high E strings. The difference in timbre creates a pleasing effect.

Example 3g

Here is another blues-rock idea. Note that the bends in bar three are blues curls i.e., 1/4 note bends, or just pushing the string slightly sharp, which creates a nice feel over the underlying Am7 chord. Be careful not to push this to a half step bend though, otherwise you'll make the chord sound like an A7, which won't work!

Example 3h

Take your time with this next idea, to accurately pin down the rhythmic shape of the line. In bar two, another blues curl that pushes the C note slightly sharp is played as an 1/8th note into two 1/16th notes. After a 1/16th note rest, the remainder of the bar is 1/16th note phrasing, apart from a fast 1/32nd note pull-off on the B string.

A fast 1/32nd note triplet phrase starts bar three. You can play this by raking your pick across the strings with upstrokes. Then we move back into 1/16th note phrasing for the rest of the line.

Example 3i

Although this next line is a very simple idea, it's worth highlighting how much we can do with just a few notes and some careful articulation. Play this line with lots of picking hand attack and add some fast vibrato. The D note that we slide into at the end is the 11th of Am7.

Example 3j

Pay attention to the rhythm and phrasing of this next line. When playing passages of 1/16th notes, rather than filling the bar with a continuous line, I find that punctuating it with 1/16th note rests has the effect of making certain notes pop out to create a punchier phrasing. Introducing a half step bend from a chromatic approach note (G# to G in bar three) is a great way of introducing a little tension to the idea.

Example 3k

Example 3l is another good demonstration of "finger painting" with the pentatonic scale across the fretboard. The line here uses only the A Minor Pentatonic scale, but in bar one doesn't sound like a typical pentatonic lick.

The fingering is a little tricky too, and requires a quick position change for the fretting hand. I think it epitomizes how I use the scale, because I'm never thinking about patterns – I'm just hearing the intervals of the scale and which is the "right" next note, because I'm so immersed in the pentatonic sound.

Example 3l

The line in Example 3m is constructed from the A Melodic Minor scale. The F# note this scale shares with A Dorian, and the G# note that sets it apart from the Dorian and minor pentatonic scales, act like approach notes in this line. The G# note leads into an A, or vice versa, creating some tension. This is also a saxophone-type line that flows continuously rather than being broken up with rests.

Example 3m

The solo ends by playing out the bridge section of the tune, covered by the next two examples.

The opening phrase here targets a C note on the high E string (the 3rd of the chord), plays the lower octave, then bends a D note (F Mixolydian scale tone) a half step up to Eb (b7 of the chord). This 6th to b7 bend is repeated in the second half of bar two. The interaction between these two notes carries on in bar three, but here we play them as individual notes rather than bends.

Example 3n

The final example begins over the EbMaj7 bar with bends from a C to D note (7th of the chord), then lands on an F (9th). From there, we anticipate the F11 chord by flowing into the F Mixolydian scale.

Using a bend with notes common to F Mixolydian and A Minor Pentatonic (G to A), we also anticipate the return to the A Minor tonality by playing a pentatonic scale phrase that resolves to A in bar five.

Example 3o

Although this solo contains some straightforward pentatonic blues language, it also contains more sophisticated harmonic ideas that don't fall under the fingers as easily. Isolate any difficult passages and work on them separately before attempting to play the whole solo.

Example 3p – "A Dragon's Tail" – Full Solo

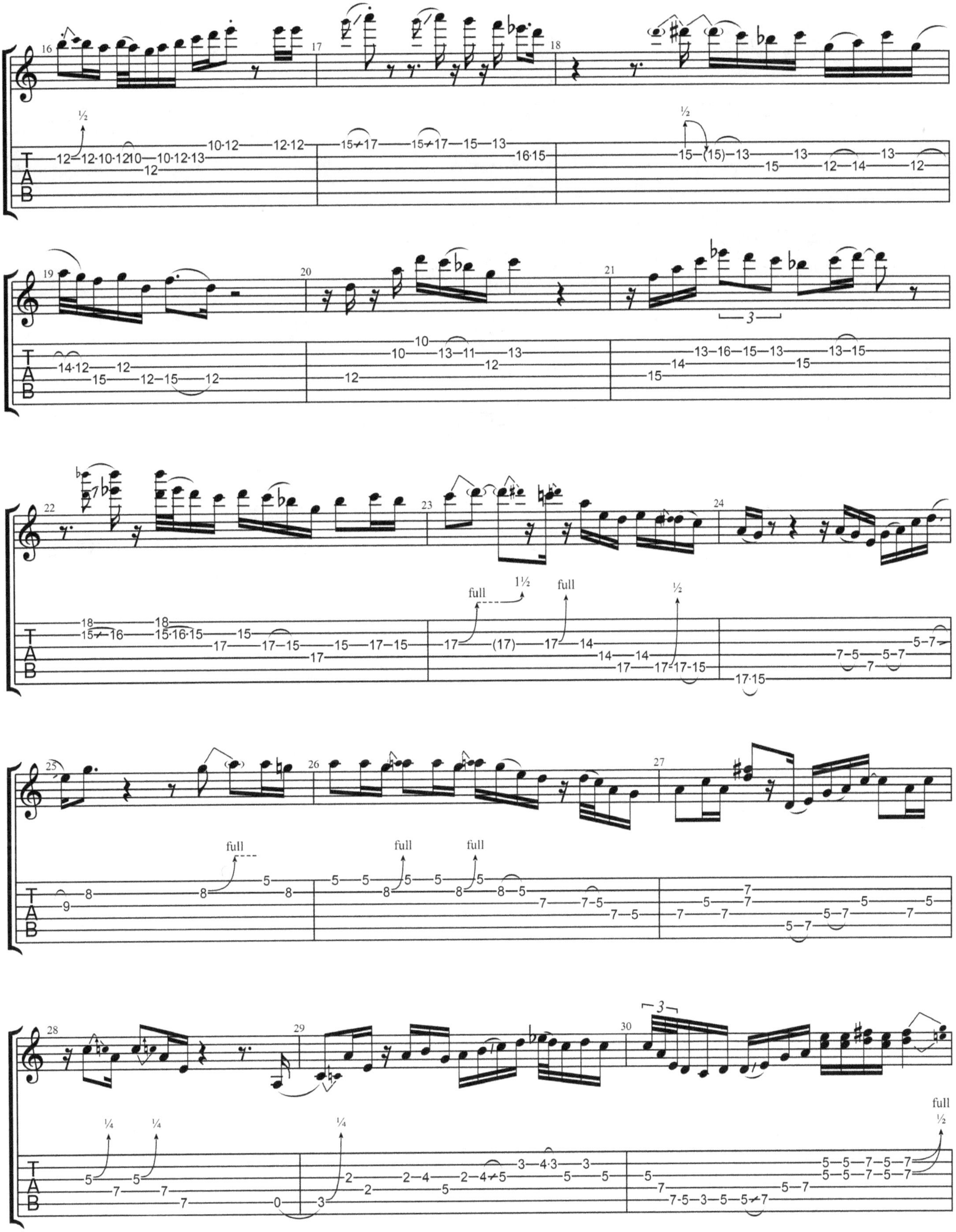
16
17
18
19
20
21
22
23
24
25
26
27
28
29
30
T
A
B
½
full
1½
¼
3

31
32
33
34
35
36
½
¼
37
38
39
full
½
½
40
41
42
full full full
43
44
45
full

This chapter has given you some exposure to moving between less predictable chord changes. To practice this idea, take any two chords and make yourself a backing track that cycles between them, playing several bars of each. It could be CMaj9 and EbMaj7, for example.

Study each chord and discover the notes they share in common:

CMaj9 (C E G B D)

EbMaj7 (Eb G Bb D)

You can see that both chords share G and D notes in common, so these are easy transition points. But notice that there are also two options for getting from one chord to the next by moving a half step (Eb to E, and Bb to B).

Now improvise over each chord and practice navigating the chord changes using one of the transition notes as a target.

Chapter Four – 7/4 Time Blues

What I Haven't Done is a tune I wrote for my album *Purple House.* Although it follows a standard three-chord blues structure, there's aren't many blues songs in 7/4 time, and I like this because it poses a challenge to our phrasing. Most blues players are used to the predictable meter of 4/4 and structure their lines accordingly, so it's good to be forced to navigate something different.

An added challenge is that it's in the key of F# Major – not a key favored much by guitar players – which forces us to go to places on the fretboard where we might not normally go.

First, a word about playing in 7/4 time signature. Each measure of 7/4 contains seven 1/4 notes. People have different ways of counting this to keep time, but the most popular are:

"1-2, 1-2, 1-2-3"

Or the reverse,

"1-2-3, 1-2, 1-2"

Go with whatever best helps you to feel the pulse.

If 7/4 is new to you, I recommend playing the chords over the backing track for a while, until you can feel the groove and know exactly when the chord changes are coming. Tap your foot along with the track to really cement the time feel.

The solo begins with an F# Minor Pentatonic (F# A B C# E) idea. In bar two, there is a bend from A to A#, which means we could also view this as the F# Mixolydian scale (F# G# A# B C# D# E).

Example 4a

Most guitar players see the Mixolydian, minor pentatonic and major pentatonic scales as interchangeable when playing over a blues, and the dominant 7 is the chord type most suited to having different tensions superimposed onto it.

We can mix and match these scales according to the type of sound or color we want to create. Here, I switch to F# Major Pentatonic (F# G# A# C# D#) for the opening phrase. When we change to the B7 chord, we're bending a G# scale tone a half step up to A, which is the b7 of B7

Bar two uses the B Mixolydian scale (B C# D# E F# G# A) and bar three flows back into F# Mixolydian. Bar three also has a whole step bend up into the 3rd of F#7.

Example 4b

The next line is the first example that shows how you might phrase a long line in 7/4 time. It combines several scale ideas, starting with F# Minor Pentatonic, flowing into F Mixolydian, and ending with the F Blues scale. This is what I mean when I say the scale choices for the blues are like colors we can blend together. We don't have to be restricted to using them in isolation. It's a question of developing your ear to hear those intervals and deciding when to use them.

Example 4c

Here's an even longer phrase that flows over the 7/4 time signature. With careful articulation, we can replicate the feel and phrasing of a vocalist, and that's what I'm aiming for here. In bar one, the half step bends from A to A# take an "outside" note (the #9 of the chord) "inside" to the safe 3rd chord tone.

Example 4d

With this next idea, over the change from the IV chord to the I chord, I wanted to play an even more vocal-like line. You can achieve a vocal quality by controlling the bends really carefully – by which I mean the accurate pitching of the note, but also the timing.

Listen to the audio and the first whole step bend over B7, and you'll hear that I bend up to pitch quite slowly, almost behind the beat. It's tempting to bend straight up to that note, but it's much more effective to slow the bend down.

Similarly, the repeated 1/4 note bends in bar two on the high E string, which bounce off a note on the B string, sound like crying or wailing when you get them right. It's actually quite a challenge to play these consistently and it might take some practice to perfect. The half step bend is bar three is also executed slowly.

Example 4e

This line begins with a chromatic walkdown to target the root of the C#7. In bar two, we're using the C# Mixolydian scale to form the melodies. At the beginning of the bar we launch the scale from the 3rd of the chord and play it in 3rds. In other words, we're not playing the scale sequentially, we're skipping every other note. The result is an almost pentatonic sounding line.

In the middle of bar two, we emphasize a root to 9th movement (C# to D#) several times, which adds some color to the harmony. This short idea becomes a motif that gets repeated in bar three.

Example 4f

In this example we're exploring more vocal phrasing. Notice that we never play two bends the same in a row here, but alternate between whole, half and quarter bends. In bar one, each time we're bending to the 5th of the F#7 chord.

In bar two, we start by targeting the 3rd (A#) of the chord. Then we move back to bending into the 5th. Strive for clarity when moving between bends, because it's easy for this to sound messy if it's not played with precision.

Example 4g

Here's a bluesy lick to navigate the IV to I chord change. You'll often hear blues players mix minor and major tonalities even within the same lick, and that's what the opening phrase does here. The bend, repeated B root note, and descending run are all F# Minor Pentatonic. Then, right at the end of bar one, we play A# to F# from F# Major Pentatonic, targeting the 3rd and root of the F#7 chord. The rest of the line comes out of F# Mixolydian.

Example 4h

This line begins with a similar idea as we use the major pentatonic scale to guide us to the target root note of C#7 and then to the 3rd. This is followed by a minor pentatonic phrase over the F#7 chord. Hopefully, by now you're really feeling the 7/4 pulse, and playing the phrase in bar two, taking a breath, then playing the next phrase over the bar line feels more natural to you.

Example 4i

Next up is a chord idea. This is probably a familiar idea to you, where we slide into the 3rd (on the high E) and root (B string) of the F#7 chord. You'll have heard this played on many blues records.

The notes we're sliding from (G# and E) represent the sus2 and b7 of the chord, but they're really just used to setup the main sound of the root and 3rd.

Rhythmically, we need to adapt this idea to the 7/4 meter. Slow this bar down and listen to the phrasing: a group of ten 1/16th notes followed by a 1/4 note rest. Then a group of twelve 1/16th notes. It's perhaps not a phrasing we would naturally play, but it fits well over 7/4.

Example 4j

If there are seven 1/4 notes in a bar of 7/4 that means there are fourteen 1/8th notes! We can count that as,

"1-&-2-&-3-&-4-&-5-&-6-&-7-&"

This line starts a fraction after beat "5&" (which is easier to think about than 1/16th note subdivisions of the bar.

In bar two, be sure to bend the F# note all the way up to G#, then release it back to sound the F# again before playing the D# at the 11th fret.

F# is the 5th of the B7 chord, while G# is the more colorful 13th, and the movement creates a nice melodic effect. Also strive for accuracy with the mixture of blues curls and half step bends that form the rest of the phrase. Remember to aim for vocal articulation that expresses emotion.

Example 4k

Here's another example of flowing between scales to express the vocabulary we want.

The first six notes here come from the F# Blues scale then, from beat 2 of bar two onwards, we're playing F# Mixolydian, and by beat 5 we're back in F# Blues.

It's helpful to look at the notation/TAB to explain what's happening in a melodic line like this, but usually I'm not conscious of playing this or that scale – I'm just trying to express the sound I'm hearing in my head.

The majority of the time I'm just listening to the intervals of the notes I'm playing and I know where the next "right" note is, guided by my ears. To close the gap between what we hear in our head and our ability to transfer it onto our instrument takes time. You just need to be willing to experiment and get things wrong before you get them right!

Example 4l

Here is a double-stop idea you can play over any dominant chord vamp for a bluesy or even country sound. Here we are using it as a motif that is carried through the line. The idea is to hold down the 5th of the chord (C#) and hammer onto the 3rd (A#) from a whole step below. Then we pull off on the adjacent string from the root to the b7.

Example 4m

This is an idea of three distinct phrases with plenty of breathing space. Again, I'm constructing ideas of a length that fit with the 7/4 time signature. First, a bluesy lick that highlights the 4th of the B Mixolydian scale.

Then, a descending phrase played in 1/4 note triplets – the effect of which is to cut across the time feel and slow things down. It ends with a slow half step bend that eventually reaches the 3rd of the F#7 chord. Lastly, an F# Major Pentatonic lick to complete the idea.

Example 4n

The last section of the solo begins with some C# Mixolydian ideas. In the phrasing there are some repeated notes for emphasis and some descending chromatic approaches at the end of bar two. The last note of bar two is actually an outside note (G) because there is a delayed resolution to the F# note that falls on beat 1 of bar three.

Bar three has another slow bend up over the F#7 chord. Normally, we've been bending into the 3rd (A#) or the 5th of the chord (C#), but here we're bending a half step into a C note, using the F# Blues scale and targeting a b5 sound. From there we work our way down to the root note to end the solo.

Example 4o

Below is the whole solo tabbed out. It's a complex one because we're grappling with the odd time signature and probably an unfamiliar key, but take your time and try and work your way through it.

If you persevere with it, you'll definitely see a marked improvement in your time and phrasing.

Example 4p – "What I Haven't Done" – Full Solo

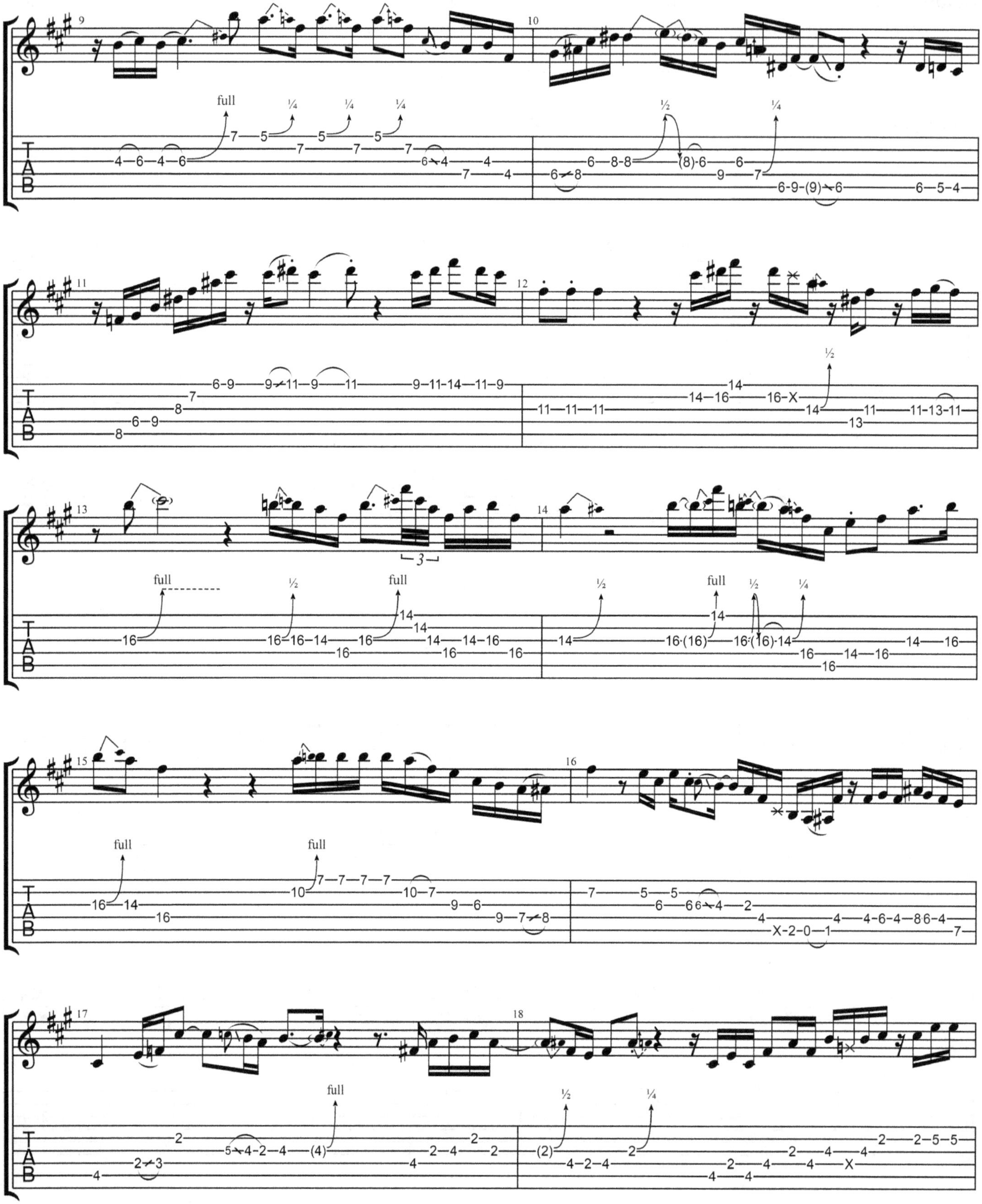

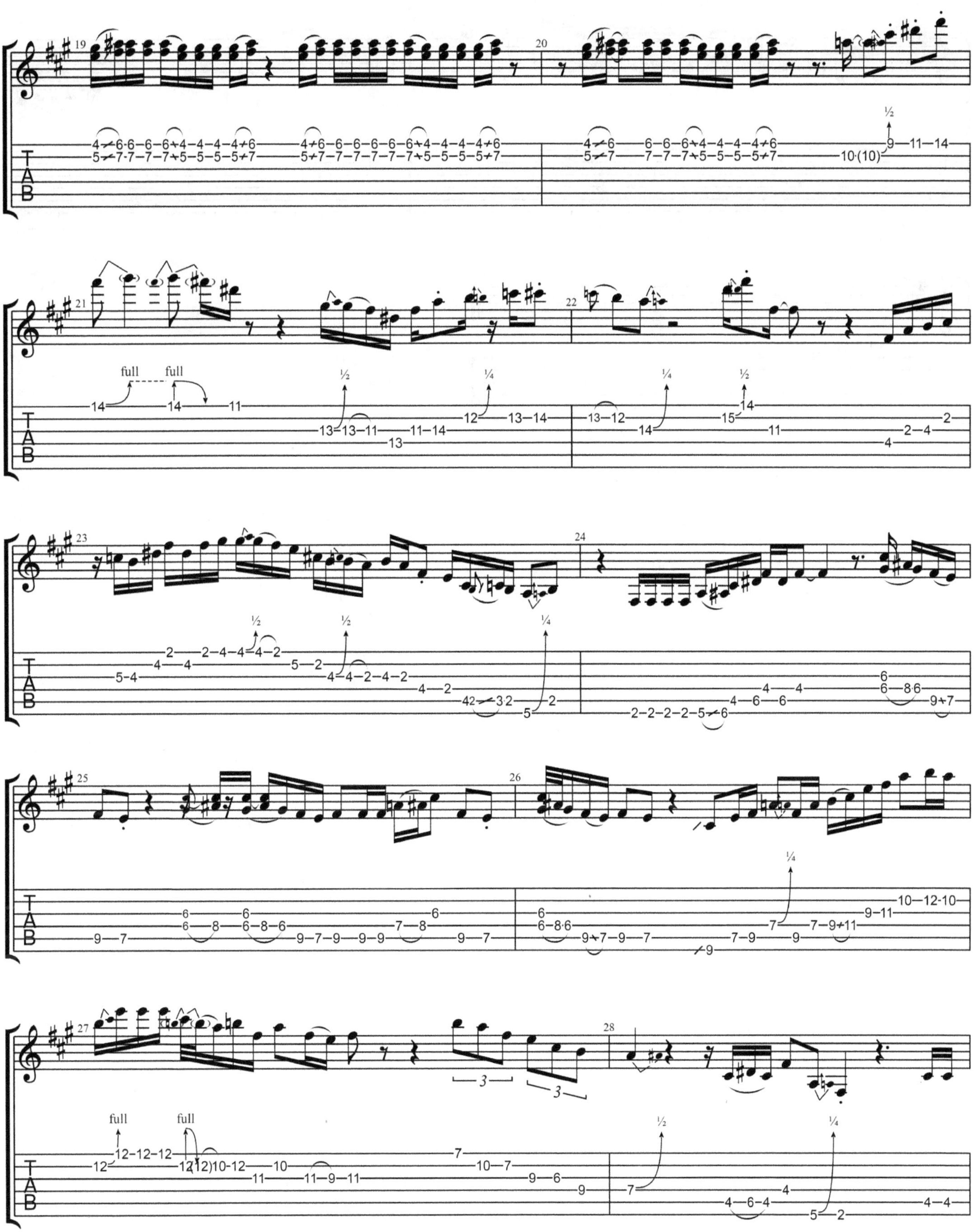
full
full
TAB
full
full

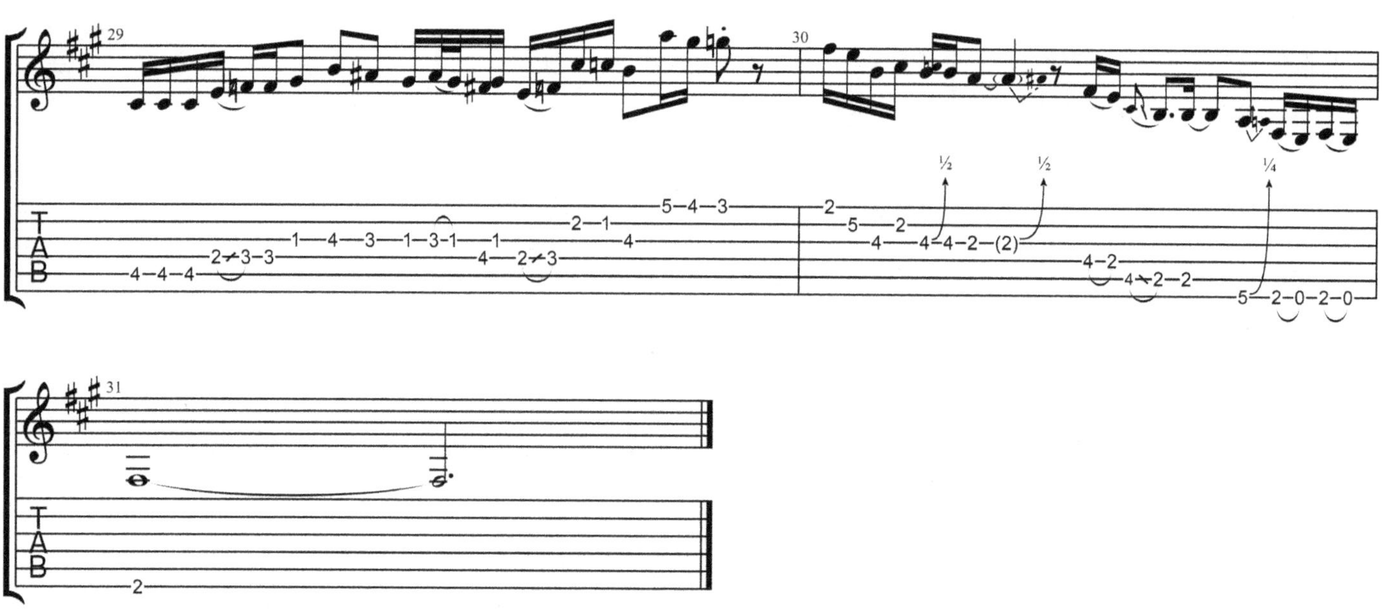
29
30
½
½
¼
TAB
31
TAB

Chapter Five – Classic Slow Blues

For the final solo, we're playing over the backing track to another tune of mine called *Blues for Lonnie Johnson* – an instrumental track written for the *Pure* album. Writing instrumental music is very different to writing a song that has a vocal melody and lyrics; it tends to bring out different things. Often, when I write, the jazz sensibility that I have starts to come out in different ways and that's true here.

This is something of a tribute to my favorite, old time, jazz-influenced blues player. If you're not familiar, Lonnie Johnson grew up in a musical family and initially played blues (winning a blues music contest which gave him a recording contract), and over time he was invited to sit in with jazz groups being recorded by the same label. He worked with Eddie Lang and became a major influence for guitarists Charlie Christian and Django Reinhardt.

We get the solo started with a line built entirely from C Minor Pentatonic (C Eb F G Bb). There are two elements to the phrasing here which you'll need to hold in tension: a relaxed, behind the beat phrasing, which needs to be combined with quick, accurate bending.

Listen to the audio example and you'll hear what I mean. Overall, the phrasing sits just behind the pulse of the music. But when it comes to the bends, you need to get them up to pitch quickly, hold the note briefly, then add vibrato.

Example 5a

The blues is all about the emotional impact of the music, and one way to inject that into your playing is by varying your pick attack and the type of vibrato you add to notes. A great deal of light and shade can be created this way.

Here, I'm using lots of pick attack and a medium speed vibrato, which results in confident sounding phrasing. Notice the slow bend in bar four, which emphasizes the fact that we're moving up to the 3rd (E) of the C7 chord. The line in bars 2-4 is built from F Mixolydian (F G A Bb C D Eb).

Example 5b

For this line, visualize a common C9 shape at the third fret with the root on the A string. The line is built around it using C Minor Pentatonic.

You already know that I don't think it terms of scale shapes, but if you prefer that approach, this is the Shape 4 box. The laid back phrasing is intended to pull back against the beat here, so don't try to play perfectly in time.

In bar two we play a short motif idea that will continue in the next example. The idea is to play the major triad of the dominant 7 chord, starting on its 3rd, then place a chromatic note above the target b7 of the chord – in this case, F# to F over the G7.

Example 5c

The two opening phrases here continue the motif. First, we play an F triad ascending from the 3rd, then place a chromatic note above the b7 of the chord. Then, we repeat the motif using the notes of the C7 chord, but we play this phrase ahead of time, anticipating the chord, so that we land on the b7 note of the first beat of bar two as the chord is played.

For the rest of this line, it's important to inject as much emotion as possible into the bends, controlling them carefully, to achieve the kind of vocal phrasing we want to emulate.

Example 5d

This section of the tune has an ascending motif idea that includes a bend. The motif begins by using the C Major Pentatonic scale (C D E G A) over C7, then bends into an Eb to target the b7 of the F7 chord.

From there, the phrasing remains the same, but the notes are from C Minor Pentatonic, bending into the 5th (G) of the C7 chord.

The motif is played again in bar three. Here, the bend from the b7 of C7 doesn't quite reach the C root note, creating some tension. We end the line with a bluesy lick.

Example 5e

The opening phrase and descending run in bar two is arranged around the common F7 chord shape we all know at the 8th fret. It uses the F Major Pentatonic scale (F G A C D) and changes into C Minor Pentatonic on the last four notes of bar two.

In bars 3-4, we're playing a simple C triad to form a chord riff, then using a repetition idea with the root and b7 of C7.

Example 5f

Spelling out chord tones is one of the simplest and most effective ways of playing through changes to clearly outline the harmony. This line begins with a straight ascending G7 arpeggio. The bend that follows targets the 3rd of F7 and a C octave phrase plays the 5th to outline the chord.

The change from F7 back to C7 is spelled out with a C Blues scale lick that lands on the C root note. The idea is repeated with different phrasing to navigate the same chord change.

Time in the practice room will always be well spent if you are just visualizing chord tones and working out different ways of getting from one chord to the next. Having a high degree of control over simple chord tone soloing will set you apart as a highly melodic player.

Example 5g

Here is another example of how you might move through the changes, targeting chord tones. At the beginning of bar two it's the b7 of C7, and at the beginning of bar three it's the b7 of F7. Then, in bar four, it's the root note of C. You can see that, often, the simplest of ideas are highly effective.

Example 5h

At this point in the tune I wanted to break things up rhythmically and do something different. The result is this 1/16th note triplet figure that utilizes the open G string. G is the 5th of C7, and the two other notes are the b7 and root note. It's harder than it sounds to pick this phrase evenly over the 12/8 pulse, so work on your timing to make it consistent.

You can pick this a few different ways, depending on your preference. Using all pick downstrokes is an option (upstrokes can work too), or using just the fretting hand fingers, with the thumb playing downstrokes on the G string and the first finger playing upstrokes on the B string.

Hybrid picking is also useful for this kind of figure – gripping the pick between thumb and first finger to play downstrokes, then using the second finger to play upstrokes on the adjacent string.

In bars 4-5 of this section, the keyboards play a common chord sequence typical of a jazz blues. After the usual two bars of the IV chord, rather than playing the I chord for two bars, chord changes are added that lead us to an A7 chord.

The principle is a simple one that has long been used by jazz musicians to make chord progressions more interesting: the idea of adding in extra ii – V movements.

Moving from Cmaj7 to Em7 (via Dm7) invites us to play an A7 chord (because Em7 – A7 is a ii – V movement and, for a split second, it's like we're playing in another key). Having played an A7, we now need a way to get to the V chord of the main key of the tune (in this case G7), so we play a Dm7 (ii) which wants to resolve to G7 (V).

You'll notice that when these chord occur, I alter my melodic line to pick out some chord tones. Over Dm7 (bar four) it's the root, b3 and b7 plus the 9th and 13th. The D note that this phrase resolves to at the beginning of bar five happens to be a shared note – it's also the b7 of Em7.

After playing the guide tones of the Em7 chord (3rd and b7), then I want to target the A7 chord. This is done by playing a jazz-style enclosure.

An enclosure just means that you have a target note in mind and play notes above and below it, before playing the note itself. Here, two non-chord tones setup playing the C# note (3rd) of the A7.

Example 5i

This example contains the ii – V resolution that gets us back to the G7 V chord. The line also begins with a sidestepping phrase – an idea we can use to create some instant tension, which is quickly resolved.

In bar two, you'll see that the first four notes played are a Dm7 arpeggio inversion, starting on the b7 and descending. The four notes in bar one are a kind of mirror image of these notes, but played ascending and moved up one fret. Sidestepping is just displacing an idea up/down a fret, then moving it into position.

Ascending a D#m7 arpeggio and descending Dm7 gives us instant tension/resolution.

You might think that this is a totally "outside" idea, and that none of the notes relate to Dm7 in any way, but that's usually not the case. More often than not, by using this idea you'll discover a mix of chord tones, chromatic tones, and extended tones.

If we break down this idea, the notes of D#m7 (D# F# A# C#) create the following tensions over the Dm7 harmony: b9 altered tone, the 3rd, the # 5, and the major 7th (which produces the most tense sound as it's a clash with the chord's minor 7th).

The main challenge in this line is the phrasing that follows in bars 3-4. Listen to the audio example a few times to get hold of the timing.

Example 5j

As we begin another chorus of this blues, the phrasing is broken up with some significant "breaths" between ideas. It's very tempting when soloing to fill as much of the sonic space as possible and ignore taking a breath. I believe the thought process behind this is to do with players feeling exposed by the silence, and feeling more comfortable when they are filling that space.

The problem with this approach is that there's no light and shade in the music; no crescendos or pauses to pull the audience in. When, in fact, leaving space and then playing something is always more interesting and engaging for your listeners.

Because we generally find it hard to leave space when playing guitar, this is the reason why some players sing along with their phrasing. If you sing what you're playing, you *have* to take a breath!

Example 5k

In bars 2-3 of this example the notes belong to the F Mixolydian scale. The phrasing speeds up slightly in bar two and the dotted 1/8th note at the top of bar three introduces a pause to make the descending run (which is straight 1/16th notes) feel more relaxed.

In bars 4-5 the extended chord changes are included again. Play through it slowly and see if you can spot for yourself which chord tones are being targeted.

Example 51

As another chorus concludes, I wanted to up the intensity of the phrasing and play with more attack, but also extend the phrases using more notes. It's so much more effective to do this having played sparser phrases with more breaths between them. If you've begun with something more melodic and measured, then the notes choices and dynamics you choose for the ideas that follow can push the boundaries more.

Over the Dm7 chord in bar one, I'm using the C Minor Pentatonic scale, focusing on the overall tonal center of the tune. C Minor Pentatonic shares three notes with C Major, so those three notes (C, F, G) sound consonant over the Dm7 chord. The other two notes of the minor pentatonic (Eb, Bb) sound dissonant and are the b9 and #5 of the Dm7 chord.

At the beginning of bar two I continue with C Minor Pentatonic. Now played over the G7 chord, the Eb and Bb notes function as different tensions. The Eb note becomes the #5 of G7, and the Bb is the #9 – both great tensions to place on a dominant 7 chord.

Next we move into a fast motif played on the top two strings. Here we've switched into the C Mixolydian scale to access the notes A, G and Eb to play a repeating phrase with notes grouped in threes.

Kurt Rosenwinkel calls a short repeating phrase like this an "energy cell", because you can move it around the neck, alter its rhythm, play it in different parts of the bar etc., and it generates a momentum that energizes the rest of the band. Yet, it remains a very simple, cellular idea that is not difficult to play.

Example 5m

If you listen to the backing track, you'll hear that at this point in the tune the keyboard player changes things up by playing a Cm7 for the I chord, instead of C7, just for the first four bars. This means we can continue soloing in C Minor Pentatonic and the notes will all sound inside.

Example 5n

Two electric blues players who made a great impact on me early in my development as a player were Albert King and Albert Collins. I don't mean to claim anything special from that, because countless players have been influenced by these two giants (notably Clapton, Hendrix and Stevie Ray Vaughan), but here's a line reminiscent of their powerful approaches to the blues.

Example 5o

This example takes us through the added ii – V movements that make the harmony more interesting to play over.

First, an ascending Dm7 arpeggio, which is added to by repeating the root then adding the 9th and 11th extended tones.

Over the Em7 chord, a little tension is added by going from an inside note to an outside one, then back inside.

Over the A7b9 chord, the movement between Bb and C notes gives us a b9 to #9 tension.

In bars 3-4, the descending line over Dm7 is quite rhythmically complex and punctuated with bends, so I recommend listening to the phrasing on the audio several times, then slowly playing your way through it until everything falls into place.

Example 5p

We end this chorus in a simple fashion by playing in the lower register, slowing down the phrasing, and leaving breathing space between the ideas. The note choices outline the chord changes. An idea like this is ideal to bring down an intense passage of soloing and it provides a kind of reset for the listener, freeing you to explore some new ideas.

Example 5q

Now we are into the final chorus of the solo. Bringing down the end of the previous chorus means we're able to ramp things up again here, and we haven't hit the listener with a constant barrage of notes!

The ascending run in bar one begins as a back-cycling pattern using C Minor Pentatonic, then switches to ascending in a stepwise motion. We continue with this scale over F7 and work our way into the top register to emphasize a Bb to C bend at the 18th fret and keep this idea going as the chord changes underneath.

Example 5r

As the chord changes to the IV chord, we keep that momentum going by reaching higher still on the top string, bending a D note a half step up to Eb (b7 of F7).

Bar two here has a long, complex line, the first half of which is played using the F Mixolydian scale. For the second half of this line, I switch into the F Half-Whole Diminished scale.

It's common to play diminished ideas launching from the 3rd of a dominant 7 chord, but you can also play the Half-Whole scale from the root to create more tense intervals. If this it too shocking to your ears when you slow it down to learn it, think of it as an outside pattern that will soon resolve back inside the harmony – dissonance to consonance. Everything is resolved when we hit that E note (3rd of Cmaj7) near the beginning of bar four.

Example 5s

As the solo comes to a conclusion, we spell out the Dm7 chord with arpeggios. For the G7 chord we're transitioning into the C Blues scale where we'll stay to close out the final chorus. Notice in bar five the four-note descending phrasing that cuts against the "three feel" of the time signature and has the effect and pulling back and slowing down.

Example 5t

Now that you've worked through the entire solo, work on piecing it together as a complete performance. Rather than resetting and starting again if you make a mistake, keep on playing and even morph into improvising your own solo if you want. Then go back and isolate/fix the areas you struggled with the previous time around.

Even if you don't end up learning the entire solo, note for note, I believe the process of working through it will have immediate benefits for your ability to construct melodic phrases.

Just enjoy jamming to the backing track too!

Example 5u – Blues for Lonnie Johnson – Full Solo

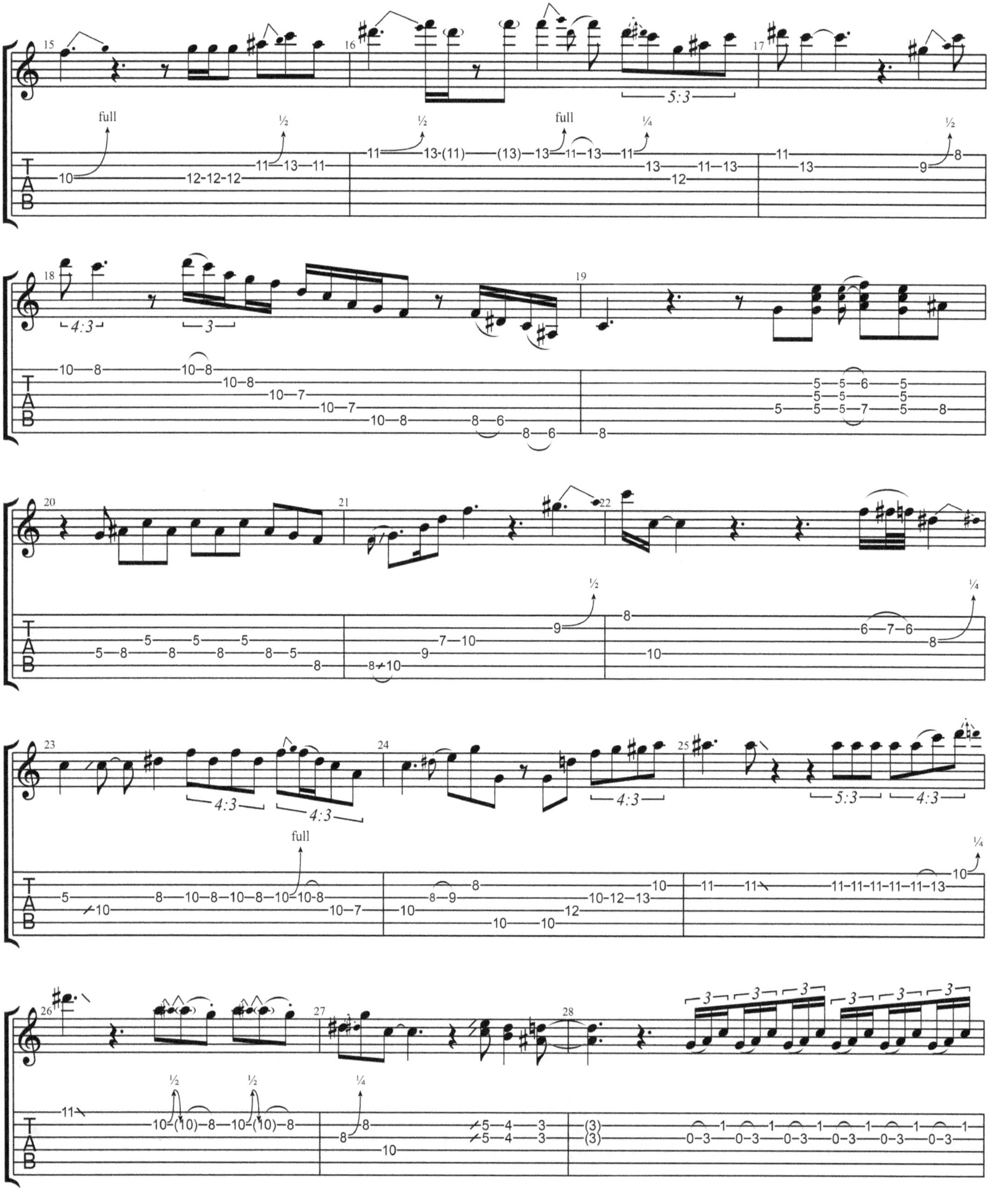
15
16
17
18
19
20
21
22
23
24
25
26
27
28
full
½
¼
5:3
4:3
3
TAB

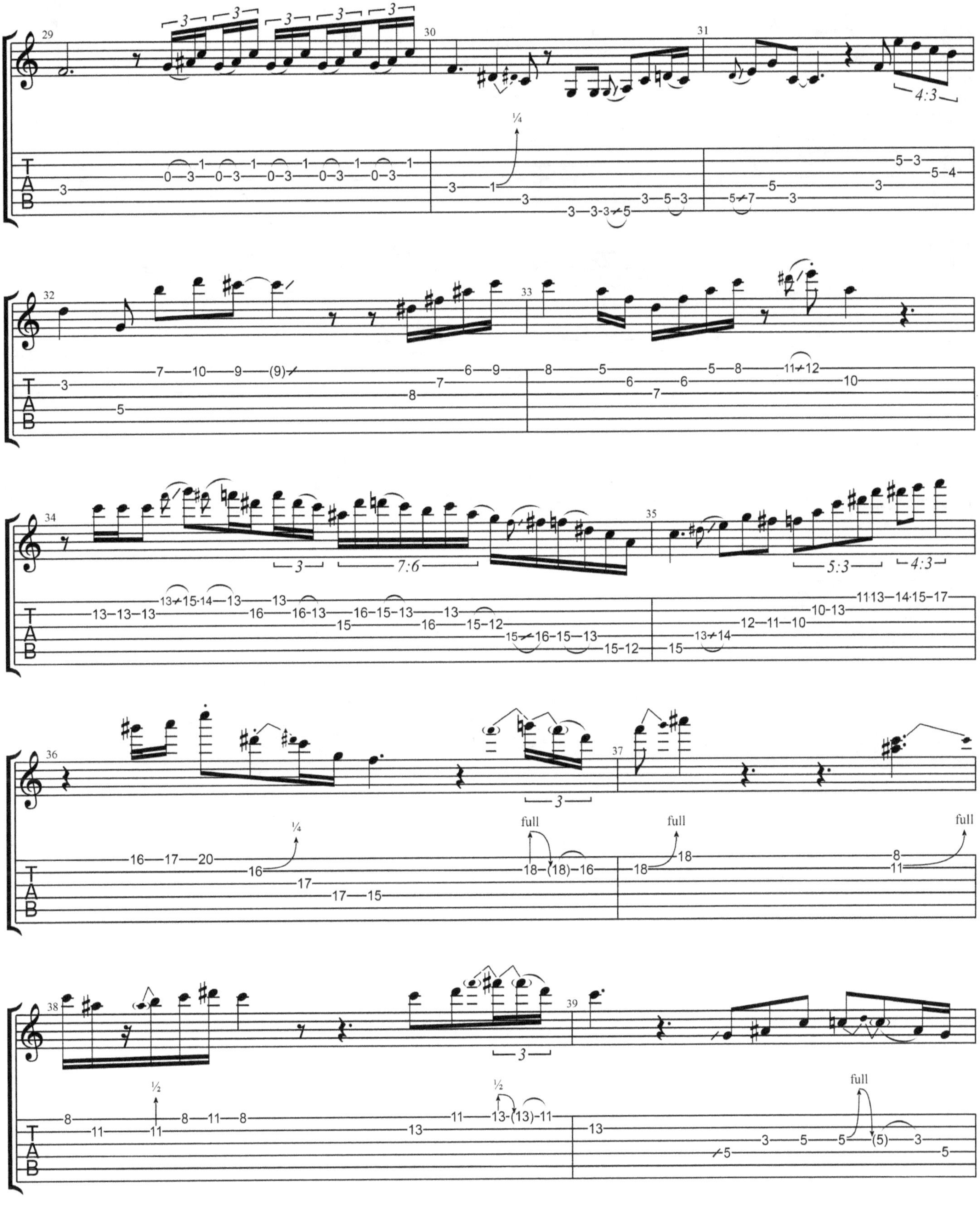
TAB
¼
full
½
4:3
7:6
5:3

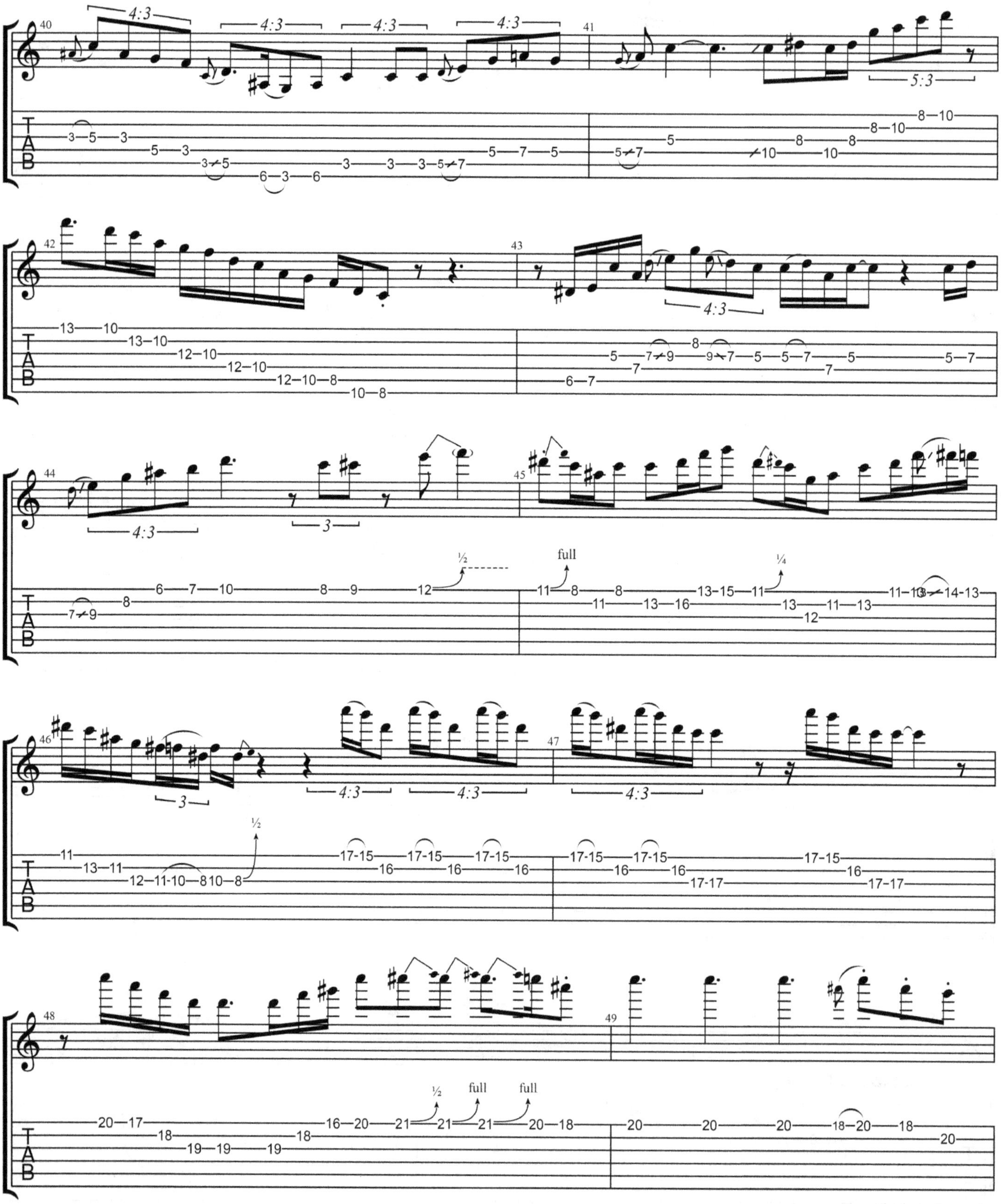
4:3
5:3
3
½
full
¼
TAB

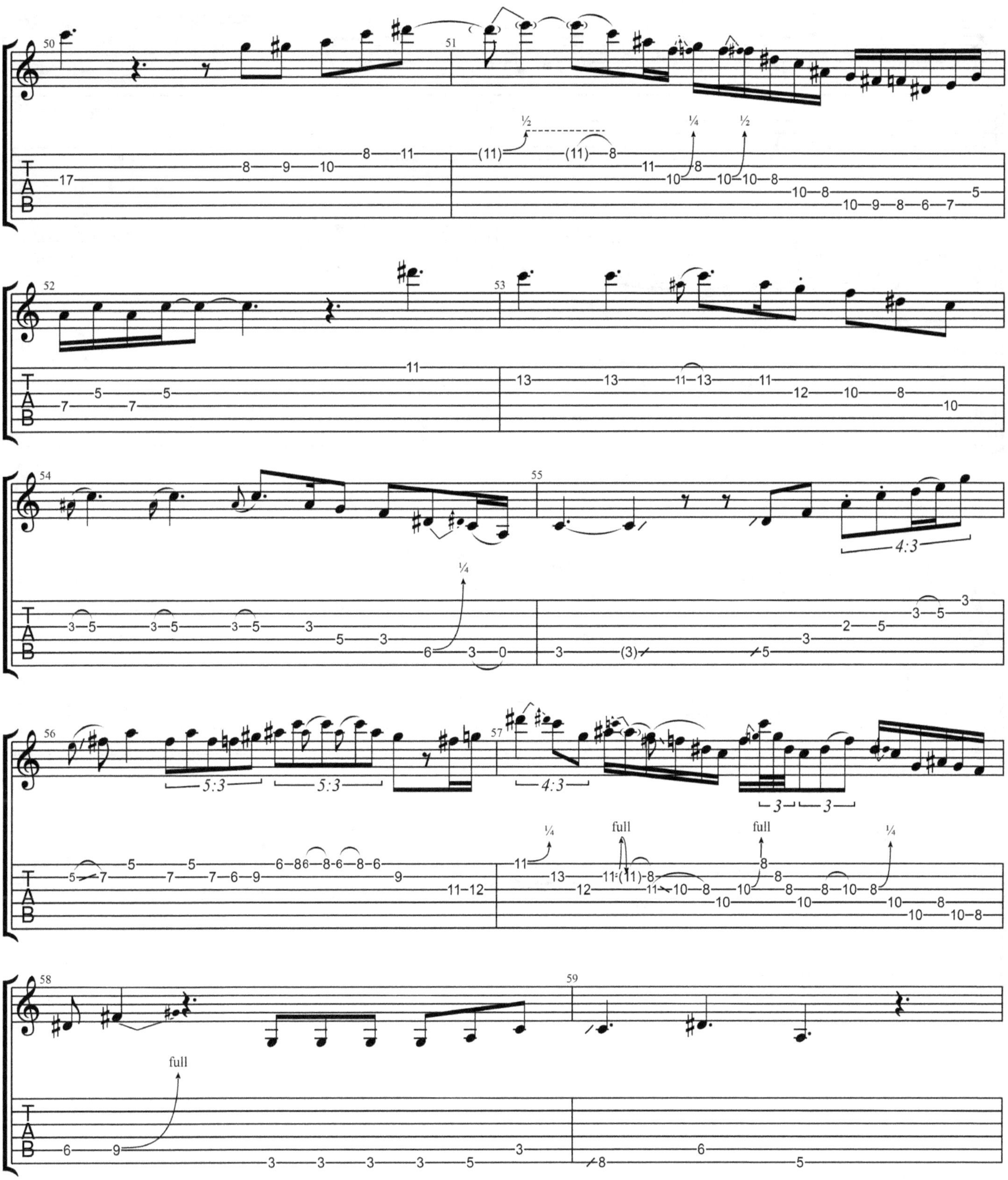
4:3
5:3
5:3
4:3
3
3
full
full
full
¼
½

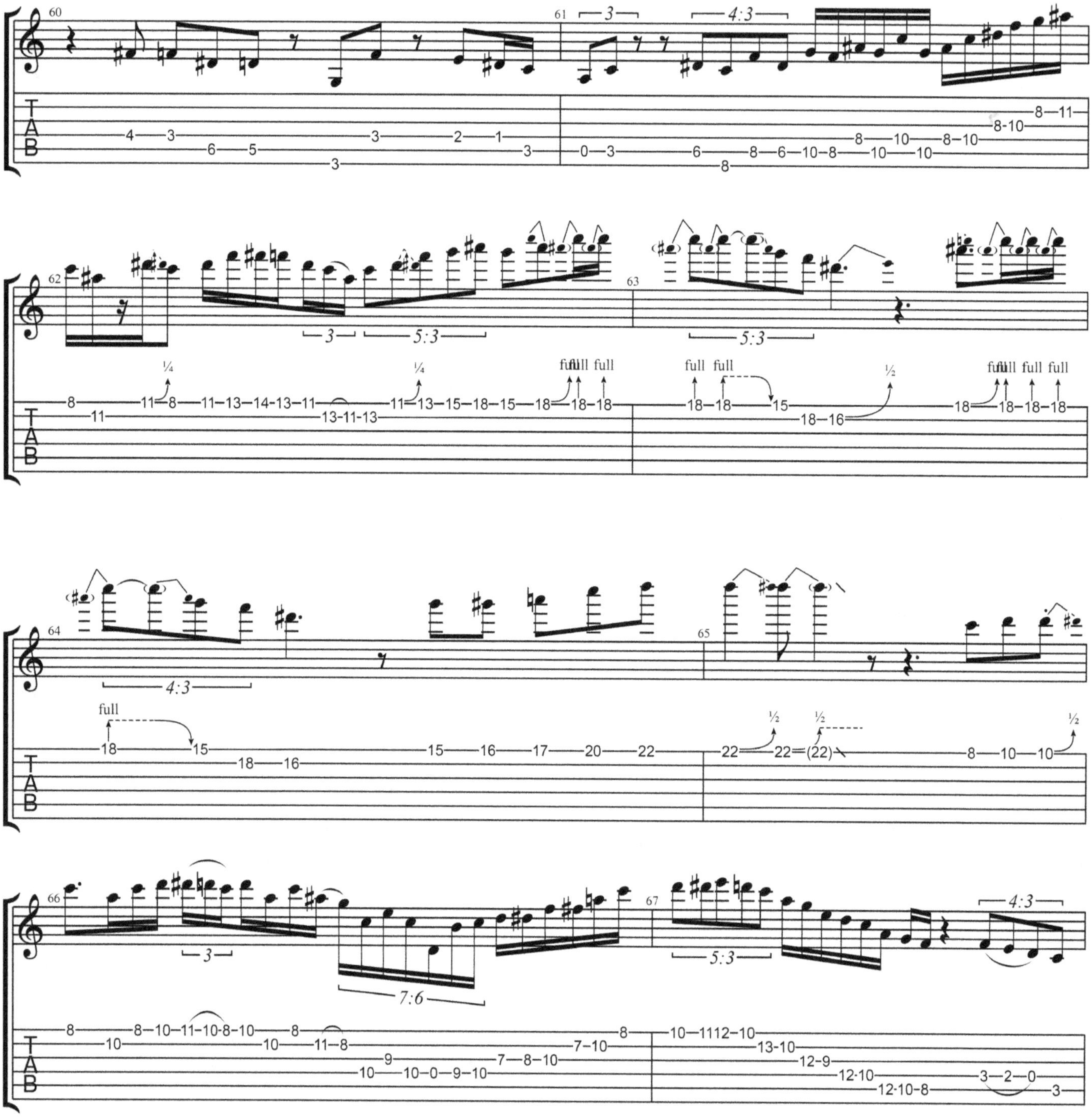

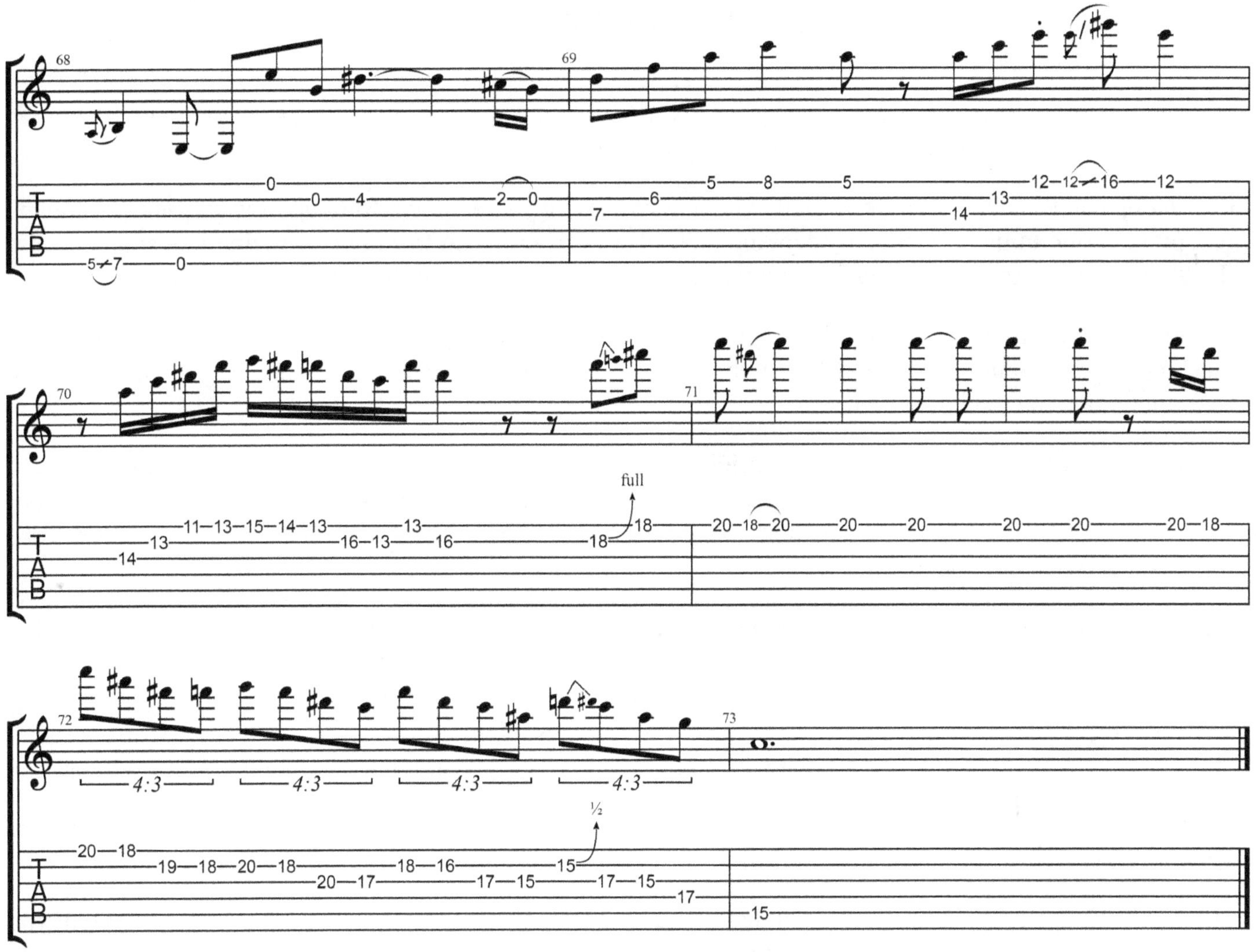
68
69
70
71
full
72
4:3
4:3
4:3
4:3
½
73

Conclusion

I hope this journey through blues phrasing has given you lots of new ideas to fuel your playing. Take these ideas and develop them. Feel free to adapt them, so that they sound more like you.

Growing up a musician, I knew early on that I wanted to find my own voice. Although I was inspired by many great players, and initially learned by copying their ideas, I didn't want to end up sounding like someone else – I wanted to find a form of expression that was uniquely me. And I want the same for you too!

We can learn a lot from books but real playing must always be a big part of your musical development. By that, I mean getting out there to play live with as many different musicians as you can – especially ones who are further along the road than you.

Early on, I was encouraged to do this by musicians who were far better and more experienced than me, and it proved a very valuable education. As soon as you play with people who are better than you, the gaps in your guitar skills immediately become apparent, and you can set about fixing them. The main thing is not to be afraid to stick your neck out and just go for it.

I've mentioned a few times throughout the book that listening is key. I think many guitar players listen to other players but don't listen to themselves very well when they're soloing. It's too easy to fall into patterns and licks we've played many times before, so a key part of your development as a musician will be developing your ear – especially hearing ideas in your head, then finding them on the guitar. Work to get to the point where, when you hear a guitarist you like play a series of notes, you can immediately play them right back.

Begin to work on these skills by playing along with the backing tracks in your audio download. You can take two approaches:

- First, work on composing a solo that has a clear beginning, middle and end. Pace your ideas so that you tell a story with your solo. Seasoned runners warm up and maybe start out with a jog before gradually picking up the pace – they don't start with a sprint. Developing a solo is the same, and this is the best way to engage your audience when you perform. You have to draw them in, then take them with you as your raise the intensity

- Second, just improvise freely over the tracks and experiment with new ideas. Try out new things and go to different places on the fretboard, away from your familiar comfort zones. Take a simple phrase and play it in as many different ways as you can. I.e. play it in different places in the bar, break it up rhythmically, play it in different zones of the neck for different timbres, introduce bends to play certain notes, and make it as vocal-sounding as you can. This work will help to close the gap between what you hear in your head and what you can immediately transfer onto your instrument

If you're interested in learning more, why not check out my Guitar Dojo at:

https://www.robbenfordguitardojo.com/

Here you'll find a supportive community of guitar players, tons of lessons, tips on technique and songwriting, advice on gear, and much more. We also have regular zoom hangs where you can ask me anything and, if you'd like, receive a personal evaluation of your playing from me.

I hope to see you there,

Robben

www.ingramcontent.com/pod-product-compliance
Lightning Source LLC
Chambersburg PA
CBHW081436090426
42740CB00017B/3325